Music
in childhood education

Music
in childhood
education

Robert L. Garretson
UNIVERSITY OF CINCINNATI

Appleton-Century-Crofts · New York

DIVISION OF MEREDITH PUBLISHING COMPANY

To Nancy
and John

Preface

~~~~~~

    This book is addressed to all those persons interested in the musical education of children—to pre-service teachers, classroom teachers, music specialists, parents, and administrators. It is concerned with the basic premises underlying instructional programs in music, with the developmental aspects of children's growth in music, with the teacher-student relationship as it affects learning, and with the ways and means to teach music effectively to children.

    The emphasis is upon specific teaching procedures for musical activities suitable for elementary school children; generalized discussions have been limited to those topics or areas necessitating this type of treatment. A chapter is devoted to each of the avenues of musical experience: singing, rhythmic activities, listening, playing instruments, and creative activities. Skills in music reading are developed out of a carefully considered program including all of the above five areas; but, because of its importance in developing the musicality of children, this topic is dealt with in a separate chapter. Part-singing is also discussed in a separate chapter to allow for a broader and more detailed treatment. The final chapter draws these activities together and deals with ways of effectively organizing the learning experience.

    In many instances grade levels are suggested for the introduction of certain types of activities. However, a specific grade level designation for the accomplishment of all skills and understandings is not always suggested because of the differences in backgrounds, abilities, and aptitudes of groups of children. Successive experiences in each area, as well as variations in approach, *are* included so that teachers will be able to give thoughtful consideration to both the *range* and *depth* of musical experiences. The inclusion of certain fundamental principles will provide teachers with a basis for adapting procedures to the unique characteristics of the particular children they will be teaching.

For students using this book in methods classes, a list of topics for discussion has been included at the end of each chapter; specific suggestions for further study have also been included for those persons wishing to delve more deeply into particular topics or areas.

Music specialists, as well as classroom teachers, may use this book as a guide in developing a comprehensive music program in the elementary grades. The classroom teacher who is inexperienced in teaching music will find within these pages many activities he can teach to children that necessitate only a minimal musical background. Classroom teachers, however, should assess their level of skills and understandings, determine those activities they *can* present and, based upon the security of these experiences, gradually widen the range of musical activities that they offer to children. It is hoped that this book will assist all teachers in this important process.

Acknowledgements

The author wishes to acknowledge his indebtedness to the many persons and firms who have contributed to this book: to Dr. Simon V. Anderson, School of Education, University of Cincinnati; Dr. John W. Worrel, Supervisor of Music, Cincinnati Public Schools; and to Mr. Robert C. McSpadden, Associate Supervisor of Music, Cincinnati Public Schools—who all read the entire manuscript and offered many helpful suggestions.

For special photographs, appreciation is expressed to the Cincinnati Public Schools; the University School, Indiana University; the Daily Herald-Telephone, Bloomington, Indiana; B. F. Kitching & Company, Inc.; Peripole Products, Inc.; and Rhythm Band, Inc.

For examples of children's creative work, I am grateful to Miss Grace Eilert, Princeton City Schools; to Dr. Nancy Nunnally, School of Education, University of Cincinnati; and to Mrs. Natalie Skurow, Losantiville School; Miss Sara McSpadden, Pleasant Ridge School; and Mrs. Joy Roof, Westwood Primary School; all of Cincinnati, Ohio.

For permission to use songs and other materials from their publications, appreciation is expressed to the following persons and firms: Allyn and Bacon, Inc., American Book Company, Follett Publishing Company, Schmitt, Hall & McCreary, Silver Burdett and Company, and Janet E. Tobitt. Appreciation is also expressed to Associated Music Publishers for excerpts from Carl Orff's *Music for Children, Bk. I, Pentatonic,* and to the Educational Publishing Corporation for examples of poems for choral speaking.

To my wife, Aretha, who typed the final manuscript and offered continual encouragement, I am particularly grateful.

—RLG

Contents

xi

Music
in childhood
education

1 Music in the modern school curriculum

From 1838, when music became a part of the curriculum in the public schools of Boston, music has gained a gradual acceptance as a part of the instructional program in elementary schools. Today it is generally recognized as an integral part of the curriculum. World events of the past decade, however, have caused educators to reevaluate the purposes, as well as the procedures, of teaching music in the schools.

The teacher of music in the modern school, if he is to be successful, must possess a well-defined philosophy of teaching. He should not only have a broad understanding of the general purposes of education, but also a thorough understanding of the specific values and purposes to be achieved by the inclusion of music in the curriculum. This understanding is essential if the recipients of the program are to reap its maximum benefits. Understanding the values of music in the education of children provides the teacher with a basis for establishing objectives that are necessary for effective teaching. In general, both classroom teachers and music specialists should strive toward the same goals. Each, however, should be cognizant of his own particular role in the school.

It is, then, toward the answering of two important questions that this chapter is directed: "What are the values of music instruction in the schools?" and "What are the objectives of music in the schools, and who is to accomplish them?"

1

Values of music in the curriculum

Many varied claims have been set forth in the past for the values of music participation, *e.g.*, "music study develops personal discipline," "music participation promotes desirable social attitudes," "singing improves posture," "music study increases one's sensitivity to beauty," and so on. These values are often used as a means of justifying the place of music in the school curriculum. While some of these stated claims deserve primary consideration, others have often been of only secondary importance and, in some instances, could perhaps better be fulfilled through other curricular areas. Some educators have been prone to accept too uncritically a myriad of reasons for the teaching of music in the schools. While it is possible for a number of values to be realized through music study, even these are of varying importance. Failure to give thoughtful consideration to the relative importance of these values has caused some teachers to lose sight of the principal objectives which underlie and guide their general approach to teaching.

Aesthetic and expressive values

The aesthetic values inherent in music must be considered the primary justification for the inclusion of music education in the schools. Aesthetics may be simply defined as the study of beauty in art and nature.[1] Man has a distinct need for beauty in his life as it serves to refine and humanize his entire being. Aesthetic education is the process of increasing an individual's sensitivity to beauty and is the primary task of the music educator.

It is important that the schools help their future citizens to become intelligent *consumers* of music. The uninformed are

[1] Beauty is a personal thing. What is beautiful to one person may not be to another. Therein lies a reason for broadening a person's understanding of the nature of music.

more likely to become victims of their own inexperience. Therefore, an important function of the music education program is
to endeavor to broaden the base of musical experiences of all
students, which should lead to a greater sense of understanding
as to the nature of music.

A teacher should never accept the standards of taste based
simply upon what a particular group initially likes best—often
jazz and popular music. This standard of taste is often dependent
on limited musical experience. The school should endeavor to
provide experiences which the students might not ordinarily have.
This means a broad experience with the finest music, which is
the cultural heritage of all citizens. The thoughtful music
educator, however, will start with music his students readily
understand. He will endeavor to explain and clarify relationships and similarities between the familiar and the new or unfamiliar. Such a procedure provides a basis for continual growth
and an ever-widening of music preferences.

Closely related to aesthetic education is the need for individual self-expression in as many varied ways as possible. Man
expresses many concepts and ideas through language, but language has its limitations. Certain aspects of man's experience are
best expressed through other media, such as the dance, the
visual arts, or music.

Each individual needs to understand himself—to create a
self-image. Each person is in the process of developing into
something, and what he ultimately becomes is dependent upon
the possibilities he envisions and the choices he makes among
them. The more opportunities one has for self-expression and
exploration of possibilities, the greater his potential for self-
development. Today's modern society needs creative individuals
in all fields of endeavor. Creativity often involves the restructur-
ing of existing components into new and useful patterns as
much as the development of the completely new element. The
development of creative individuals is, in part, dependent upon
ample opportunities for exploring possible solutions to problems
in all curricular areas. Music and the other arts can offer varied
possibilities for the expression of individual feelings in a creative
manner.

Cultural and personal-social values

An important function of the school is the passing on to future generations of our Judeo-Christian heritage which has developed over hundreds of years. Music, of course, is an integral part of the total culture. It is a part of Man's worship service, governmental and military ceremonies, and is used to enhance the effectiveness of dramatic productions presented through the media of radio, television, and motion pictures. Some music has a soothing and tranquilizing effect and for this reason has been used effectively by industry and in shopping centers and hospitals. It has been used to stir emotions at political conventions, and as a means of developing group cohesiveness and singleness of purpose at various other types of meetings. Music as a force in American life cannot be ignored.

The objective of world peace is dependent to a very great extent upon an understanding of other cultures in addition to our own. Music is an integral part of all cultures and the hopes, fears, aspirations, and beliefs of various ethnic groups are often expressed through their folk music. Complete understanding of these peoples cannot be achieved unless all aspects of their cultures, including music, are included in the units of study taught in the schools.

Certain personal-social benefits may also result from music study. Although highly important, they cannot be considered as the primary values to be achieved by the study of music because these benefits may also accrue from other studies in the curriculum.

It is important that all individuals develop a feeling of self-assurance. This comes about through having a variety and number of successful school experiences. It is a fundamental responsibility of all teachers to assist children toward finding their own strengths so that such self-assurance may be attained. Perhaps some individuals will excel in music, while others will find different fields more rewarding. To best meet the needs of all students the schools should provide a variety of experiences —including music—in the curriculum.

Some writers have endeavored to justify the inclusion of music in the curriculum on the basis of its physical benefits. Actually the over-all physical development of students may best be achieved through planned activities in physical education. Nevertheless, habits of correct posture and proper abdominal-diaphragmatic breathing may accrue from experience in vocal and instrumental music.

During a normal school day various tensions are bound to build up within students in the classroom. These tensions result in fatigue and prevent students from accomplishing their desired goals. The cathartic values of music participation have long been known. Music activities, as well as art and physical education, when interspersed between various academic subjects can result in a lessening of these tensions and may effect the necessary atmosphere conducive to continued academic work.

The development of social beings able to take their places in adult society is another responsibility of the entire school. Participation in music activities may contribute toward this end. While some classrooms and rehearsal rooms have a more autocratic than democratic atmosphere because of the personalities of the teachers, the music class, because of the nature of the subject, does lend itself toward the development of various social values. The effective teacher can develop attitudes of cooperation, attitudes which also are necessary for a competent performance of the music being studied. Acceptance by peers is highly important to the personal-social development of youth. The importance of individual skills and cooperative group effort needed for the success of musical organizations provides a social setting for the development of mutual respect and new friendships.

Elected student officers of musical organizations should work cooperatively with their director in the establishing of policies and the implementing of plans. Such opportunities for student leadership responsibility contribute to the social development of the students involved. Policies and plans may be submitted to the group-at-large for approval. The will of the majority is followed, yet the opinions of the minority are respected. Such experiences in the democratic process are valuable and necessary in preparing students for later adult life.

Avocational and vocational values

Avocational interests, those outside a chosen occupation, serve to enrich one's life and renew one's spirits from the tensions and frustrations encountered in everyday life. Avocational choices will, of course, vary widely according to the needs and interests of individuals. Music is a particularly attractive avocation because persons of all ages may participate. A look into the future would probably reveal a greater use of automation in industry and a subsequently increased amount of leisure time. Therefore, the schools should provide ample opportunity for experience with a variety of types of possible avocational choices.

If the music in our culture is to be perpetuated, then children must be provided ample opportunity for exploring this area as a possible life's work. To be successful in the music profession one must develop certain basic skills and understandings. Therefore, children should have the opportunity to begin their musical studies relatively early in life.

Relationship of values
to type of activities

The aesthetic values of music are paramount in an educational program in the schools; but these values may not necessarily be of central importance when music is used in certain social situations, such as, in adult community sings, or at summer youth camps. In these instances the primary function of the music leader is not merely to instruct, but to use music as a force in creating group cohesion, esprit de corps, or perhaps a recreational atmosphere. This does not necessarily mean that the song leader must lower his musical standards. It simply means that he will often be using music of a different type toward achieving a different type of goal.

Formulating objectives of music education

What is an educational objective? An objective is a goal or an end toward which one strives. Without carefully considered objectives the teacher is hindered in the planning of appropriate classroom experiences and his teaching is likely to be ineffective. Being only vaguely aware of what he hopes to accomplish, a teacher may have some success. However, considerable time may be wasted and the students will lack the appropriate educational experiences to stimulate, challenge, and develop their potential to the greatest extent.

Evaluation is an integral aspect of the educative process and is a continuous on-going process. Periodic evaluation of student progress is essential to continued growth. "Why haven't the students learned this better and what are ways to improve their understanding of certain concepts and ideas?" Teachers should continually ask themselves these questions and develop means for determining answers. However, if evaluation is to be effective, such questions must be framed and answers determined in light of certain stated goals or objectives that are established prior to the teaching of each lesson.

There are two basic types of goals or objectives—general and specific. General, or overall objectives, are roughly equivalent to the values of music stated in the previous section of this chapter. Specific objectives are those skills and understandings that the teacher hopes his students will accomplish on a particular day.

The successful formulation of general objectives is dependent upon a well-developed philosophy of education, which will result only from considerable reading and reflective thought.[2] Varying points of view as to desirable objectives will be en-

2 For background material on "The Selection of Objectives for Education in American Society," see Ralph L. Pounds and Robert L. Garretson, *Principles of Modern Education*, New York: The Macmillan Company, 1962, Chapter 8.

countered by the avid reader of educational literature. To be
most effective in practice, the values of music participation must
be translated into statements of what the teacher hopes to accomplish. Little benefit will be derived from simply reading
some other person's or group's stated objectives. To be meaningful they must be carefully considered and expressed by each
individual teacher. Of the many values to be derived from music
participation, the following are given only as examples of how
a set of general objectives for music education might be stated.

1. To develop in children an awareness of and a sensitivity
   to the aesthetic aspects of music in our culture.
2. To help children become intelligent consumers of music
   by increasing their understanding and appreciation of
   music of varying types.
3. To assist children toward achieving their fullest potential
   by expressing particular feelings, concepts, and ideas
   through music.

The development of general objectives by the individual
teacher of music will serve to clarify and refine his thinking
and will be a guide and motivating force in the planning of
various classroom experiences. In the preparation of each music
lesson the teacher must also give careful consideration to
specific objectives, or what he hopes to accomplish on that
particular day. Specific objectives are a necessary part of each
lesson plan and should precede any detailed statement of
activities and procedures which the teacher plans to use as a
means of accomplishing his stated objectives. Following are
several examples of specific objectives which the teacher might
strive to accomplish on a particular day:

1. To develop an improved concept of the technique involved in singing music in a legato style.
2. To develop an improved understanding and rhythmic
   responsiveness to the dotted note.
3. To teach children to recognize the Rondo form and to

develop an understanding of this form as an expressive device utilizing the principles of unity and variety.

Who is to teach music?

After consideration of the values of music and the objectives we wish to attain, we come to the matter of who is to teach music in the elementary school. Who is to implement these objectives? What are the roles of the music specialist and the classroom teacher and what is the nature of their relationship? Schools vary in their answers to these questions. The following arrangements, however, are most common.[3]

1. The classroom teacher. In schools organized around the concept of the "self-contained classroom," the classroom teacher generally has the responsibility of teaching all the subjects, including music. The teacher, knowing the needs, abilities, and interests of his particular class, is thus able to integrate music with the on-going class activity and make it a meaningful learning experience. Unfortunately, these teachers do not all possess the necessary background and skills for teaching music adequately. As a means of meeting this problem some teachers have assisted each other in the teaching of subjects in which they feel insecure. One classroom teacher, for example may teach all the music to several classes, while another will teach art, and perhaps still another physical education. Thus the strengths of each teacher are used to the best advantage. While at least this comprises a workable arrangement, it cannot be said to be a widespread practice. Teachers who enjoy music and see its values, and who feel adequate in teaching it, will employ it whenever possible and appropriate. Those who feel inadequate about teaching music will shy away and sometimes totally ignore it. Under this

---

3 Cf. Edward J. Hermann, *Supervising Music in the Elementary School*, Englewood Cliffs, N.J.: Prentice-Hall, Inc., 1965, pp. 3-4; and Robert E. Nye and Vernice T. Nye, *Music in the Elementary School*, second edition, Englewood Cliffs, N.J.: Prentice-Hall, Inc., 1964, p. 8.

arrangement, therefore, programs in music instruction may range from the adequate to the practically nonexistent.

2. *The special music teacher.* In some elementary schools, where the administration feels a special music teacher is necessary and desirable, a person especially proficient in music—usually with a Bachelor's degree in music education—will have the major responsibility for the teaching of music. Of this arrangement, quite a wide variation in practice exists. In some situations, the person may be simply a traveling music teacher, perhaps visiting on a rotational basis a number of schools. The teacher's schedule generally allows him to visit each classroom periodically, with lessons ranging from twenty to thirty minutes in length. The frequency of the visits is dependent, of course, upon the number of schools and classrooms for which the teacher is responsible. In certain instances, the relative infrequency of the teacher's visits, because of a heavy teaching load, makes the visitations barely worthwhile. In school systems with adequate finances, and where an adequate number of teachers are employed for the task, satisfactory results may be expected. To teach music adequately, however, sufficient time must be provided for both planning and teaching. For a teacher to move hurriedly from classroom to classroom, without giving consideration to the on-going class activities and the needs and interests of the students, generally negates the values of the visit.

In other situations, one teacher may be assigned to a single school, with the responsibility for teaching all the music from grades one through six. In some instances the teacher will make regularly scheduled visits to each classroom. In others, the children (generally only those in the intermediate grades) will move to a special music room for instructional periods of varying length, depending upon the local school situation. Under this arrangement, many teachers keep themselves well-informed as to the nature of the work in the children's other classes and endeavor to correlate their material whenever possible. In still other schools, the music specialist may teach only those students in the intermediate grades, with music instruction in the primary grades being the responsibility of the classroom teachers.

3. The music consultant and the classroom teacher. Grow-ing out of the administrator's recognition of the necessity for good working relationships, as well as the most prudent and economical use of the music specialist's time, is the trend toward the increased use of the position known as the *music consultant.* In this approach the responsibility for the teaching of music is a cooperative endeavor between the music consultant and the classroom teacher. The function of the music consultant is to aid and assist classroom teachers toward growth in professional competence. Underlying this approach are the administrator's beliefs that classroom teachers *can* teach music, that classroom teachers are in a unique position of correlating music with other classroom work, that music ought to be a part of the daily ex-perience of children rather than simply a twice-a-week activity, that most teachers will need some special help if the total program is to be effective, and that the music consultant does possess a unique background which enables him to give special help to those teachers who need it. The use of music consultants has been successful in many communities, particularly where the administrator has carefully clarified the nature of the re-sponsibilities of both the classroom teachers and the music con-sultant.

The music consultant may assist classroom teachers in many various ways. He may travel to a number of schools on a rotational basis for the purpose of visiting the classrooms of teachers who need and request assistance in their teaching. (Some classroom teachers are highly competent in the teaching of music and need only a minimum amount of help.) The specialist may observe a lesson and offer suggestions. It must be understood that the specialist provides aid because the classroom teacher requests assistance with her teaching and not because of a quasi-administrative responsibility. This is the key to effecting working relationships. The specialist does not prod the class-room teacher, but serves as a resource person, ever ready to give needed assistance. Whenever the teacher-consultant relationship is good, the consultant may give a demonstration lesson in the classroom and perhaps launch the music aspect of a particular unit of study. Perhaps the classroom teacher, in planning a new unit of study, needs suggestions on appropriate materials. The consultant with his broader background and reference library of books, music, and recordings, can provide invaluable help and assistance.

Workshops in the teaching of elementary school music can be most helpful to classroom teachers. Such workshops might be scheduled twice monthly, perhaps for an hour and one-half after school. When teachers are cognizant of their needs and interested in improving skills and understandings, these sessions can be highly beneficial. Teachers should participate wholeheartedly in all the activities which they expect to teach their children. This will, of course, include experiences in singing, rhythmic activities, listening, playing instruments, and creative activities. Music skills and understandings are accomplished best by *doing* and not by simply talking about them.

Topics for discussion

1. Why is it important for teachers to have a well-defined philosophy of education?

2. In what ways is music an "end," and in what ways is it a "means" to an end?

3. Compare the functions of the classroom teacher, as regards music teaching, with the music specialist. Indicate the specific desired contributions of each to children's musical development.

4. Discuss the importance of educational objectives as they relate to the quality of the learning experience.

Suggestions for further study

ANDREWS, Frances M. and COCKERVILLE, Clara E. *Your School Music Program: A Guide to Effective Curriculum Development.* Englewood Cliffs, N.J.: Prentice-Hall, 1958, Chs. 1-5.

COMBS, Arthur W., Chairman, ASCD Yearbook Committee. *Perceiving, Behaving, Becoming: A New Focus for Education.* Washington, D.C.: Association for Supervision and Curriculum Development, 1962.

ELLISON, Alfred. *Music With Children.* New York: McGraw-Hill, 1959, Ch. 1.

HERMANN, Edward J. *Supervising Music in the Elementary School.* Englewood Cliffs, N.J.: Prentice-Hall, 1965.

HOFFER, Charles. *Teaching Music in the Secondary Schools.* Belmont, Calif.: Wadsworth, 1964, Ch. 2.

LANGER, Susanne K. *Feeling and Form.* New York: Scribner, 1953, Chs. 1-3, 7-10.

LANGER, Susanne K. *Philosophy in a New Key.* New York: New American Library, 1948, Ch. 8.

LEONHARD, Charles and HOUSE, Robert W. *Foundations and Principles of Music Education.* New York: McGraw-Hill, 1959, Ch. 4.

MURSELL, James L. *Developmental Teaching.* New York: McGraw-Hill, 1949, Ch. 10.

MYERS, Louise Kifer. *Teaching Children Music in the Elementary School,* 3rd ed. Englewood Cliffs, N.J.: Prentice-Hall, 1961, Chs. 8 & 9.

POUNDS, Ralph L. and GARRETSON, Robert L. *Principles of Modern Education.* New York: Macmillan, 1962, Ch. 8.

2 Experiences in singing

Singing is a very natural and emotionally satisfying childhood experience. Very young children are often initially exposed to singing through a mother's lullaby or by hearing the informal singing of other members of the family. Presentation of a variety of types of songs commensurate with the child's level of comprehension is an integral and important part of the many morning television programs designed for children of pre-school age. Learning to sing is initially an imitative process and most children learn to do so quite as naturally as they learn to speak. Singing is also as natural a form of personal expression as speech and young children may often be observed singing to themselves—singing simple songs they have learned and which appeal to them, and even expressing various thoughts, however brief, through song. An increasing number of children today attend nursery or pre-schools for one or two years prior to the time they enter kindergarten. A most important objective of these schools is helping the children to learn to work co-operatively together and to develop self-confidence. Music activities, and singing in particular, become important means for achieving these objectives and should be an integral part of the school's activities. Children, therefore, do enter the elementary school with a certain amount of background experience in music, however varied it may be. It is important for the teacher to realize this and to understand that children should not be ex-

14

pected to accomplish beyond the limits determined by their physical maturity.

The child voice

Hearing the myriad of vocal sounds on an elementary school playground has caused some observers to wonder about the type of voice quality which teachers should strive to develop in children. Actually there should be no doubt. In practice, teachers can develop almost any quality they strive for, because the human voice has an inherent flexibility which enables it to "imitate" a variety of types of sounds. The vocal mechanism of a child, however, is smaller than that of an adult and lacks the maturity and development which occur through continued use and training. The question then remains, what quality is most

Cincinnati Public Schools

Music for very young children is informal and intimate.

natural and characteristic of the child voice? In the author's opinion, the proper quality should be light, clear, and flutelike. It may even be described as ethereal in nature. This does *not* mean to imply that children's voices should always sound like angels', because certainly in the interpretation of a song the voice quality or color may and should differ to the extent necessary to reflect the moods of the music. But it does mean that children's voices should be kept reasonably light in quality and the heavy, darker quality characteristic of mature voices should be avoided. Even with adult singers, the development of a dark, heavy voice quality, when not sufficiently supported by the breath, will result in flatting, an excessively wide vibrato, and other intonation difficulties. The problem, of course, is more acute in children's voices because of the lack of bodily strength and the general lack of development of the entire vocal mechanism. Therefore, if satisfactory results are to be obtained in singing, the child voice must necessarily be kept light and flutelike in quality. It is often helpful to think of lining the child voice on the o͞o vowel. Even some vocalization on this vowel will be helpful in developing the concept in the children's minds of the voice quality that they should be striving for. Various teachers have also found it helpful to differentiate between two types of voice qualities—the type used on the playground and that used for singing.

The voice range of the young child is somewhat limited. This fact must be understood if the teacher is to select songs that will not prove harmful to children's voices and that may be sung with a reasonable degree of ease. The old axiom that the range of children's songs should lie within the treble staff is applicable for children in the intermediate grades, but not for very young children. While some children in the kindergarten and first grade may have a voice range from G below middle C to fourth space E, many others who have not yet completely discovered how to use their voices may have, for example, a range of only a fifth, from first line E to third line B. Initial songs for kindergarten children should therefore be selected with this latter group in mind. As children grow in their vocal capabilities, songs with more extended ranges may be utilized.

Suggested pitch range for songs in
a.) Kindergarten-primary grades, and
b.) intermediate grades

It should be understood that the voice range increases gradually as a result of both bodily maturation and vocal training. Obviously, no abrupt changes in range can be expected to occur between the third and fourth grades, or between any grades. Vocal development in some children may be considerably ahead of the group and others may lag behind the average. Even some whole classes may be found to be ahead of others on the same grade level.[1] Therefore, as a necessary means of encouraging the optimum development of the children's voices, teachers should be careful to select songs well within the range limits of the majority of the group. Songs with extreme range may have a detrimental effect upon their voices and are not conducive to expressive singing.

Most of the songs found in the basic music texts have been carefully selected in consideration of the musical capabilities of the students, as well as their interests and the units of study generally undertaken at each particular grade level.[2] Teachers using these tested materials may still encounter a few difficulties, but the authors of each series *have* endeavored to consider the problem of range, as well as difficulty, in preparing the books for each grade level. However, when songs are obviously too high for a particular group, they may be lowered in pitch a half or a whole tone. It is generally unnecessary and often undesirable, however, to lower the pitch of these songs more than a whole step. Certainly the development of the high range will not be facilitated if children are not encouraged and given ample opportunity to sing in a high, light head-voice.

[1] Factors determining this difference may be the amount of singing experience, the type of training, and the teacher's voice quality and attitudes toward music.

[2] A list of basic music texts for the elementary grades is included in the Appendix, pp. 252-54.

The *tessitura,* or "average range of a song," is actually a more important factor to consider in selecting a song for a group than is the occurrence of an occasional high or low note. If the tessitura of a song is too high, then undue vocal strain may occur, the expressive qualities of the music may be lost, and the development of the children's voices may be hindered.

The voice range of some teachers is limited and some, therefore, make the mistake of lowering the pitch of a song to a key a third or more below the given pitch of the song merely to suit their own convenience. It is really grossly unfair to ask an entire class to adjust to the vocal limitations of one person. Rather, the teacher should adjust to the natural range of the children. Considering the somewhat restricted range of young

Cincinnati Public Schools

Proper posture is necessary to the achievement of good tone quality.

children in particular, the majority of teachers can make the necessary adjustment with a little effort.

Teachers should endeavor to sing with a light tonal quality, as the heavier chest tones of the adult voice are not easily carried into the upper register. Since children are likely to imitate the voice quality of their teacher, the proper model of a light, flutelike quality (in so far as is possible for the teacher) will facilitate the development of the child voice. As an aid in lightening the voice it is suggested that teachers vocalize periodically on the ōō vowel, attempting to keep the voice light and the resonance high and forward.[3]

Teaching procedures

Since in the initial stages of musical development children learn songs through an imitative process, usually called rote learning, it is essential that teachers utilize good tone quality and proper diction. Appropriate tone quality, as discussed in the preceding section, should be light, with the heavy quality of the chest register being avoided. As regards diction, care should be taken to pronounce correctly all words and to enunciate them in a clear, distinct manner. A generalized American approach to pronunciation should be followed, and when in doubt about particular words a dictionary should be consulted. Clear enunciation is dependent upon the precise articulation of the consonants in particular; the teacher should concentrate upon the exact movements of the articulating organs, *i.e.,* the tongue, lips, teeth, palate, and the lower jaw.[4] Clear enunciation is usually facilitated when the teacher exaggerates the lip movements in presenting a song to the children. Careful attention to diction is important if children are to hear and understand the words of a song, for the rapidity with which the song is learned

[3] For a discussion of resonance in the adult voice, see Robert L. Garretson, *Conducting Choral Music*, Second Edition, Boston: Allyn and Bacon, Inc., 1965, pp. 86-93.

[4] *Ibid.,* pp. 103-107.

is dependent to a certain extent upon the children's understanding of the words.

The whole and phrase methods

The actual performance time of songs selected from basic music texts for the elementary grades will vary from between twelve to sixty seconds. Songs for very young children are generally quite short—sometimes only two phrases in length. Songs for older children, of course, will be longer and some may have a number of verses. In teaching rote songs a teacher may use one of two procedures: a whole song approach, where the children hear the entire song and repeat it after the teacher; or the phrase method approach, where after hearing the entire song, the children repeat each phrase after the teacher. Of course, the whole song approach is utilized primarily for songs which are shorter in length, whereas the phrase approach is utilized for songs which are longer and more difficult in nature. However, what is difficult for one group may not necessarily be difficult for another. Factors which determine the teacher's choice of method or approach are the length and difficulty of the song, the children's previous musical background and experience, their basic musical aptitude, and the motivation and interest which they possess in regard to the song. Specific steps in these two methods are outlined as follows.

Whole song method.

1. Motivate the song through the use of appropriate pictures, stories, or questions.
2. Ask the children to listen for something specific in the song prior to its actual presentation.
3. Present the song to the class.
4. Ask questions about the student's understanding, or enjoyment, of the song.
5. Sing the song one or more additional times, depending upon the group's readiness to participate.
6. Have the class join in singing the song.

Phrase method.

Steps 1 through 5 are the same as in the whole song approach. When children are ready to join in (step 6), the teacher sings one phrase at a time and the children repeat each phrase after him. After each phrase has been sung, the complete song should be sung at least once from beginning to end.

Regardless of the approach used, it is important that the teacher motivate the song in some appropriate manner, whether it be by showing pictures which evoke interest, telling a story, or simply asking the class questions about their interests which might lead to a discussion of the general subject of the song. The purpose of the motivation is simply to focus the students' attention upon the topic to be studied in order that the most desirable learning situation be created. Motivation need not be lengthy, but should be direct and to the point. When the singing of a song grows out of a topic or unit of study, then the need for motivation is lessened and may be shortened considerably.

Prior to the teacher's initial presentation of the song, he should ask the class to listen for something specific in the song as he sings it. The teacher may do this by telling the class to "Listen carefully while I sing the song, because afterwards I am going to ask you some questions about it." This request should never be made in the form of a command, but more in the manner of sharing a special secret with the class. After the song has been presented the teacher should ask the class some specific questions about the words in each phrase. Teachers will want to give careful thought to the phrasing of these questions so that the desired response will focus the group's attention upon the central thought in each phrase. This is important because a clear understanding of the ideas involved in the song will facilitate the learning of it.

In questioning the children about various aspects of the text, the teacher should insist that they raise their hands. This eliminates, to some extent, the mass mumbling effect of group answers. While a group response is justifiable in some instances, it is generally more desirable to allow only one student at a time to answer the teacher's questions. In this way, the students are more likely to listen for and hear each other's responses. It is also desirable for the teacher to strengthen the idea by paraphrasing each student's response. The child's answer, coupled with the teacher's embellishment, allows the children more opportunity to grasp the concepts in the song.

If, after the teacher's initial presentation of the song, the children are unable to answer or discuss particular questions pertaining to it, he should repeat the singing of the song one or two additional times. In each instance, the teacher should ask the class to listen again for the answer to a particular question. Even when children can answer all questions about a song correctly it is not too likely that they will be able to sing the melody with any degree of accuracy after only one hearing. Therefore the song should still be repeated one or more times. The actual number of repetitions will depend upon the length and difficulty of the song, the children's previous musical background, and their ability to grasp new concepts. Prior to each repetition, the teacher should provide the class with a reason for doing so. After the initial presentation, it is desirable in some cases to ask questions about the first two phrases only, with the remaining questions being asked following the repetition. In the event children display a reasonable degree of understanding of the words the teacher may have the class focus their attention upon some technical or appreciative aspect of the music. An appropriate direction for younger children might be, "Listen for the highest note," or "Listen for the points of rest." Older children might be asked, for example, to listen carefully and count the number of phrases in the song. Finally the teacher asks the children to join him in singing the song and, depending upon the factors previously discussed, will use either the whole or phrase approach. Actually, in practice, a teacher may wish to use a combination of both approaches. That is, his initial presentation might be through the whole approach, but then, after the children have sung the song once or twice, he may want to attack in a phrase-method approach certain musical problems, such as faulty singing of certain intervals or inaccurate rhythmic patterns.

Using recordings

A considerable number of the songs in the basic texts have been recorded; sets of records are available for each grade level and may be obtained from the publishers. These recordings may be effectively utilized in the presentation and study of songs. Of course, the teaching procedure followed must of necessity be the whole song approach; instead of singing the song, as in steps three and five, the teacher would simply play the recording. The other steps in the whole song approach should be followed as suggested. (See p. 20.)

Recordings of songs in the basic series have proven extremely helpful to classroom teachers. Many teachers who feel somewhat inadequate about the teaching of songs have been able to implement a reasonably successful singing program without possessing any outstanding degree of vocal skill. Some teachers have utilized recordings as a means through which they learn the songs, in order that they personally may be able to present them to their classes. Of course, this self-improvement is a most desirable step for teachers to take, for they will be able to make the songs more meaningful and enjoyable to their students than can ever be possible through the use of a recording. This does not mean to minimize the value of recordings. They can serve as an enriching musical experience. Being able to listen to a professional rendition of a song will often assist the children in the development of a broader musical perspective.

Recordings are also helpful to music specialists for the same reason, *i.e.,* broadening the student's musical horizons. Also, they may be of help to classroom teachers and music specialists alike when they are unable to use their voices adequately because of a cold or laryngitis.

Getting started

Two problems involved in beginning a song are those of establishing the proper pitch and the correct tempo. Both are of some concern to the beginning teacher and should be given careful thought.

Establishing the pitch.   All teachers should possess a pitch pipe and, of course, learn how to use it properly. The fundamental purpose of the pitch pipe is not only to provide the correct pitch for the teacher, but for the children as well. Occasionally the pitch may be given by means of the piano or some other readily available instrument; hearing sound in various media can be a helpful and beneficial experience for children. However, the quality of the pitchpipe, if properly blown, is generally easier for the children to hear and the pitch is easier to match. In addition, a pitchpipe may be easily carried in one's pocket and is always conveniently available for immediate use. The same cannot always be said for the availability of other instruments. Initial teacher experiences with the pitchpipe sometimes result in two tones rather than one being sounded. This somewhat embarrassing problem can be avoided if the teacher will place the thumb immediately below the tone opening to be played and bring the thumb up to the mouth. Before blowing, the lips should be puckered slightly and breath directed into the instrument in a relatively narrow stream. In providing the pitch for children, the tone should be sustained for a reasonable length of time and short puffs should be avoided. The teacher should remember that the pitch is not only for himself, but for the children as well.[5] A pitch pipe has one thing in common with other instruments—a certain amount of practice is essential to achieve a desirable tone quality. Therefore, the teacher should possess a definite familiarity with the pitchpipe before attempting to use it in the classroom.

    [5] A generally accepted practice is for the teacher to play the tonic pitch or keynote on the pitchpipe, then sing the tonic chord followed by the beginning note.

Establishing the tempo. When in doubt about the correct tempo of a particular song, the teacher is advised to study carefully the text. A thorough analysis of the words will reveal the basic mood of the song, and this has a direct bearing on tempo. In addition, he should recite to himself the text of the song, as the rhythm of the words coupled with the overall mood will dictate the most desirable tempo. Other factors, such as the maturity and musical backgrounds of the children should also be taken into consideration. However, these should be considered subservient to the dictates of the rhythm of the words and the overall mood of the song.

In teaching a song, the teacher should prepare the class for its beginning and establish his desired tempo by utilizing the phrase, "Ready, sing!" These two words should, if possible, be sung on the beginning pitch of the song and in the desired musical tempo. In songs of 4/4 meter, for example, if the music begins on the first beat of a measure, the words, "Ready, sing!" should be spoken precisely on beats three and four preceding the first note of the song.

In addition to preparing the group with verbal commands, it is also desirable for the teacher, particularly in the intermediate grades, to use a preparatory conducting movement.[6] These movements are illustrated in the following chapter on rhythmic activities. It is not suggested that elementary school teachers conduct the entire song they are teaching, but rather only a measure or two, primarily for the purpose of helping the group to get started and to help establish the tempo. In the initial stages, the experience of watching for the conductor's movements, and listening for the verbal command, serve to reinforce each other and tend to make each more meaningful. As the students become more alert to the teacher's conducting movements, however, the verbal directions of "Ready, sing!" may be gradually eliminated. In addition, the teacher may assist the group in starting by a slight nod of the head and through appropriate facial expresisons. All

[6] For a detailed presentation of the basic conducting movements, see Robert L. Garretson, *Conducting Choral Music,* Second Edition, Boston: Allyn and Bacon, 1965, Chapter 2.

of these movements combined provide the best preparatory movements for the children.

Maintaining rapport

Teacher-student rapport is most readily attained when the teacher establishes eye-contact with the students in all parts of the room. This is best achieved through slow, casual movements of the head and body. A few steps taken toward one side of the room, a pause, and a return to another part of the room also improve rapport. Teachers should avoid a rigid, stationary position as it can quite conceivably give the impression of boredom or simply lack of enthusiasm—certainly not desirable traits for any teacher. Facial expressions reflecting the overall mood of a song may also contribute to improved rapport.

Other teaching considerations

Whether the teacher utilizes the whole or the phrase approach to the teaching of a song, it is generally advisable to present initially the complete song to the class in order that the children may develop a concept of the whole song. With this concept in mind, the class is better able to relate the parts, which they hear and study, to the whole song. However, in teaching songs with an extensive number of verses, this practice generally should not be followed. It is best to consider the "whole" in this case to be one complete verse, rather than the total of all the verses. As the class usually has a strong desire to participate, it is generally advisable to allow them to do so as soon as possible. Once the class has adequately learned the rhythmic and melodic patterns of the song, the learning of additional verses becomes a relatively easy task. In short, be sure the students know the "tune" before introducing additional verses.

In songs involving the repetition of words and/or phrases from previous verses, such as encountered in the song "Mac-

Donald's Farm," difficulties often stem from confusion over the order of the repeated words. In such songs, learning can be facilitated by printing the entire word series on the chalkboard prior to the initial presentation. Students can then follow the visual patterns of the word progressions while the teacher sings and much unnecessary confusion may be eliminated. This procedure may be used from approximately the second grade on, depending, of course, upon the student's ability to read and understand the words which the teacher has written on the chalkboard. If the song is used for some recreational purpose, however, then the amusement which comes from the sometimes natural confusion over words may be justified. In such cases the teacher may prefer not to use the above suggested procedure.

In teaching action songs there is sometimes a question as to when the teacher should introduce the actions. Should it be during the initial presentation of the song, concurrently with the melody, or after the students have learned the melody and words? There is no single answer to this question. The proper procedure will vary according to several factors—namely, the length and difficulty of the song, the nature of the actions, and the children's concentration abilities. In some songs, learning simple actions concurrently with the music often facilitates the learning process, as the motions serve to pinpoint and reinforce the retention of the important or key words.[7] In other instances, teaching the actions too soon may distract the student's attention from the music and certain melodic and rhythmic patterns may be learned incorrectly or, at least, will take a longer time to be learned correctly.[8] The question, therefore, is whether the actions add or detract from the music. To determine the answer the teacher should carefully consider all the previously mentioned factors.

[7] An example of a song in which the actions may facilitate the learning of the music is "The Teapot," *The First Grade Book*, Boston: Ginn, 1949, p. 7.

[8] An example of a song in which the suggested actions may hinder the learning of the song is "The Bus," *Singing on our Way*, Boston: Ginn, 1959, p. 153.

Assisting the uncertain singer

Some children "find" their singing voices sooner than others. In the past this rather natural occurrence has caused no end of concern to classroom teachers, as well as to some special music teachers. In discussing and conferring about these children, teachers have used various terms such as "monotones," "non-singers," and "out-of-tune singers," as well as "uncertain singers." The first three of these terms reflect, in general, a somewhat negative attitude toward the problem. The term "uncertain singer" is definitely the most descriptive of the children's problem as well as being a more precise one. Some persons have advanced the idea that certain children are incapable of learning to sing. This may be true only of deaf children and those with serious speech defects. Any child with normal speech and hearing can learn to sing—not always expertly, but at least adequately.[9] Viola Brody states that, "Every child who has a larynx, which functions in speech, can learn not only to perform vocally, but to perform with a pleasing quality." [10]

Causes of difficulty

If teachers are to assist children in "finding" their voices they must be cognizant of the causes of the problem. An adequate understanding is essential to the development of and maintenance of the proper attitude, as well as for providing a basis for the continual exploration and implementation of various means to assist each child toward the fulfillment of his own potential. In general, a child's difficulties may stem from one or more of the following causes.

[9] There are even cases where children with less than normal speech and hearing have been known to develop limited singing ability.
[10] Viola Brody, *An Experimental Study of the Emergence of the Process Involved in the Production of Song,* unpublished Ph.D. Thesis, University of Michigan, 1947, p. 78.

Physical immaturity.   It is generally understood that some boys and girls physically develop sooner than others. This fact is quite obvious when one observes the differences in height, weight, and bodily coordination of any group of first grade children. More careful observation is necessary to note that some children are able to focus their eyes upon the printed page more readily than others. Their inability to use the singing voice properly may, likewise, stem from lack of physical development. This lack is no more unnatural than, and is often related to, the immaturity of the rest of the body.

Lack of experience.   Children come to any given first grade class with a variety of backgrounds of experience with music. Some have attended nursery school for one or more years, others have had the benefit of possessing and listening to their own record collections. While many children have had the opportunity to listen to children's programs on television, not all will have maintained the same degree of interest, nor reaped the same benefit from them.

Psychological blocks.   Some children have developed psychological blocks, or "negative sets" against participation in music activities in general, and singing activities in particular. Such negative sets generally occur because of some unpleasant experience with, or associated with, music. Perhaps the attitude on the part of the child was caused by some biting or sarcastic remark made by another child, or by some type of behavior on the part of the teacher. Children's negative sets may be caused by one, or perhaps by a combination of several factors. In any case, the child "retreats" within himself because of fear—fear of being unsuccessful, or of being ridiculed. Rather than attempt to sing the child convinces himself that he is unable to do so and, therefore, exhibits behavior accordingly. Sometimes the child's fears are real and sometimes only imaginary. Whatever the case, his musical development is stunted, and he is unable to make further progress until his attitudes are changed and he achieves some degree of self-confidence.

Often the attitude of the teacher has a very direct bearing upon the development of positive attitudes toward music. The teacher who is understanding of children's problems, and who strives patiently toward helping each child develop toward his maximum potential, will have a minimum amount of such "singing" problems in his class.[11]

Some years ago it was in vogue for teachers to seat their students near the piano in three rows for the singing lesson. The best singers were placed in the last row, in order that the other children might reap the benefit of hearing their "in-tune" voices. An intermediate group of children, who posed some problems but whose singing was generally satisfactory, was placed in the second row. The children having various vocal difficulties were placed in the front row near the teacher, where he could provide them with the maximum amount of assistance. In theory this idea seems feasible and in some instances proved practical and helpful. In other situations, however, the procedure caused quite negative results. Problem situations usually developed when teachers, probably for the convenience of a quick seating arrangement, assigned various names to each group. Often the name of a particular bird was assigned to each group. The "superior" group in the last row might have been called "canaries," the intermediate group in the second row might have been called "robins," and the problem group in the first row was given some other bird's name. For all practical purposes, it might as well have been "crows," because this is the self-concept that this group of children developed about their singing abilities. The author has discussed this problem with many hundreds of in-service teachers. Many recall that they were the "crows" and still remember the stigma that was attached to this system of grouping. Many attribute their present singing difficulties to this early experience with music. Fortunately, the grouping system described above is not particularly prevalent today. It is given as an example, however, of an undesirable learning situation and a classroom atmosphere unconducive to effective learning. While teachers may not group children as previously described, they may likewise contribute to the development of

[11] For a further discussion of negative sets see Ralph L. Pounds and Robert L. Garretson, *Principles of Modern Education*, New York: Macmillan, 1962, pp. 59-63.

negative attitudes toward music by various unguarded remarks or by facial expressions which express impatience, non-approval, or even disgust. It is, therefore, absolutely essential that teachers carefully examine their own attitudes toward music, and endeavor always to utilize a positive attitude in dealing with children.

Tone-matching devices

Various tone-matching devices may be used as a means of helping young children to match particular pitches more accurately or to sing various intervals more readily. Tone-matching devices will be found to be most effective when they grow out of the on-going class activity. Thus, a natural means of motivation is provided, with the children highly interested and engrossed in the total learning experience. Tone-matching devices may grow out of a variety of classroom situations, but, perhaps the most natural approach is to relate them to particular songs. The following example is illustrative of one approach.

Following the class' singing of the song, "Three Little Kittens" (from *Music 'round the Clock,* p. 56, Follett Publishing Co.), the teacher might say, "Boys and girls, our kittens in this song seem to get into all sorts of difficulty. I suspect they are the kind who might wander away from home and get lost. If the kittens really were lost, their mother would worry, and perhaps call to them, so they might find their way home. *Let's play a game!* I'll pretend that I am the mother cat and you are the kittens. When I call "meow," you will answer back on the same pitch! So all our kittens won't be answering at the same time, I will point to some of you one at a time. We may not have time today for all our kittens to answer, so some of you will have your chance another day." [12]

[12] A suggested approximate pitch for this tone-matching device is F (first space, treble clef), however, the actual pitch should be varied according to each child's vocal range. Herein lies the value of the teacher knowing well the capabilities of each child. If the teacher can select a pitch which the child may most readily match, then his confidence may be developed and his singing improved.

The purpose of tone-matching devices is, of course, to assist children to learn to more adequately use their singing voices. The teacher, then, should begin with the group of children who have the most difficulty, and concentrate upon them. However, all children in the class should periodically have the opportunity to participate in such activities. It will not only be beneficial to the child who has "found" his voice, but will serve to support the teacher's real purpose for using tone-matching devices, which is to assist those children having difficulty. This is important because young children in general do not like to be different, nor to be singled out of a group for any purpose. The children who are having the most difficulty are in many cases likely to be slow developers, sometimes shy and reticent as well. The addition of too much obvious pressure may only add to their adjustment problems and they may withdraw or retreat further into their world of inactivity in which they feel safe from criticism.

The humming sound (as in "meow") is easily produced by the children and is a good beginning point. However, infinite possibilities for tone-matching exist and should be utilized. For example, children might "moo" like a cow, "hoot" like an owl, howl like the wind "ooo . . . ooo . . . oo," "squeak" like a mouse, or "baa" like a lamb. The "tick-tock" of a clock and "toot-toot" of a train are other possibilities. Some kindergarten and first grade teachers prefer to call the morning role by singing each child's name and requesting an answer on the same pitch. The falling minor third is common to the experience of most children, having been called on this interval by their parents or by other children.

Another approach to tone matching would be simply to select appropriate intervals from particular songs. For example, the following intervals might be utilized after the singing of any song about bells.

Still another approach is to ask the children to match the pitches of particular instruments as they are played. The added experience of hearing and matching pitches of varying timbre can contribute substantially to the child's musical development. Instruments that may be used are the melody bells, the Flutophone or Tonette, the piano and, later, any of the band or orchestral instruments that the teacher may play adequately. Although not a musical instrument as such, considerable benefit may also be derived from the children matching various pitches which the teacher might play on the pitchpipe.

Regardless of the type of motivation, pitch or particular interval, the timbre or quality of sound which the teacher utilizes for tone-matching, three basic principles apply to their use and each should always be given careful consideration.

1. Establish rapport.   The teacher should endeavor to establish rapport with each child. It is helpful to move to a position relatively close to the child and attempt to "personalize" this musical experience. Initial responses are likely to be somewhat subdued, and to adequately hear the child the teacher must be reasonably close.

2. Adjust to the child's pitch level.   The teacher should select a suitable pitch level for each child (based upon familiarity with the child's background and previous musical experience). Utilizing tone-matching devices in the approximate middle range of the child's singing voice will generally facilitate the successful accomplishment of an accurate response. When, however, a child is unable to match the teacher's pitch and invariably responds on a higher or lower pitch, the teacher should immediately select the child's pitch in singing any subsequent notes or melodic patterns. In other words, it is best to select the pitch of the child's first response. After a reasonably accurate response is achieved on this pitch, the teacher may then sing his next pitch or pattern just a bit higher or lower. In this manner, the child is met at his own level, and he is provided an experience with which he can more likely achieve some degree of success. Such a feeling of accomplishment and success provides a desirable attitude and motivation for such future learning experiences.

3. Be positive in your remarks.   The advice, "accentuate the positive," certainly applies in dealing with young children as well as with other individuals. A teacher should always reassure the child concerning his progress. Some children, when not meeting success, are likely to become discouraged. Often a series of unsuccessful experiences sets up a barrier in the child's mind against future effort. The child may think to himself, "I just can't do this, so why try!" The teacher plays a vital role in the development of the children's attitudes. His facial expressions, tone of voice, and what he says all have a definite effect upon the child's opinion of his own worth. In addition to assuming a sympathetic, understanding attitude, a teacher should utilize such remarks as, "That's better! Now just a little higher!"

Establishing the concept of tonal direction

When a teacher, in assisting a child to sing more accurately, says, "Sing a little higher," or "Sing a little lower," some children may be unsure of his directions and, because their concept of tonal differences has not yet been established, will be unable to follow his advice. This concept, sometimes called tonal direction, is seemingly quite elementary to older children and to adults, while to the young child with limited musical experience it can be a great discovery. A clear understanding of this concept is an important step in the musical development of all children. Some children, as a result of their general experiences in music, seem to assimilate this concept very readily and without any deliberate effort on the part of the teacher. Others, and the uncertain singers in particular, need to have particular attention paid to clarifying this concept. This may be done best through a series of musical experiences designed for and appropriate to the achievement of this objective. In the initial activities, the child should learn to identify the differences between *high* and *low* tones; the extremities of pitch are a suggested beginning point. Later, subsequent learning activities will enable the child to differentiate between more subtle differences, such as various tones in the musical scale. Some suggested procedures and activities for establishing and clarifying this concept are as follows.

Relating the concept to meaningful childhood experiences. In developing a clearer concept of high and low tones the teacher should begin with ideas or concepts which the child has experienced and readily understands. For example, the teacher might relate, again, the story of "The Three Bears." In telling the story, he should utilize a *high* voice when describing the baby bear, a *medium* pitched voice for the mother bear, and a *low* voice for the father bear. Point out pitch differences to the class, if necessary, then play a game: talk in voices of varying pitches (*high, low* and *medium*) and see if the class can identify the particular "speaking" bear in the story. It is also helpful to identify the high and low voices of various children in the class.

Another approach would be to sing or imitate contrasting sounds which they hear in everyday life. For example, ask the children to sing up *high* like a little train whistle ("too—too—"), and then down *low* like a big streamliner train ("whoo—whoo"). Still another approach might be to draw on the chalkboard a scene to depict the ground, a fence, and the sky. Discuss these height differences with the class, as low, medium, and high. Next, ask the class to sing various phrases on the syllable pitches *do, sol,* and *do:* "down on the ground" (*do*), "up on the fence" (*sol*), and "high in the sky" (*do*). The concept may be made even more meaningful by subsequently asking the class to use appropriate bodily movement while singing. On the first phrase, the class should squat down touching the floor, on the second phrase they should stand almost erect, and on the last phrase they should stand on tip-toe and reach "high in the sky."

Using visual and aural devices. Utilizing a visual or aural device of some type may assist children in the development of the concept of tonal direction. A good beginning point is for the teacher to play for the class on the piano some simple tune, in its normal and originally designated pitch level. Then, the teacher may play the tune an octave or two above the original tonal level, and then an octave or two below. Comparing the "high" and "low" versions to the original, he may ask which tune sounds higher and which sounds lower. The children may then be allowed to experiment on the piano. Selected students may be asked to play some "high" notes and some "low" notes.

Utilizing various simple musical instruments, such as the five-tone marimba and the melody bells, as a part of the class work will also assist both visually and aurally in the development of this concept. Tuned water glasses may also be used for this purpose. The resonator bells may be effectively utilized to facilitate tonal awareness in somewhat older children. The teacher may select eight bars (in the diatonic scale) and distribute them to particular children in the class. The group may then be asked to sound their respective pitches and to try to form the scale by lining up in the front of the room with the lowest pitch to the left and the higher pitches to the right. An orderly procedure must, of course, be followed and the teacher will ask pairs of children to compare pitches before taking a definite place in the line. The class may also be asked to give their judgments as well, especially if the participating children have difficulty in making the comparison.

The teacher may also assist the child by using the visual device of placing the hand in various positions between the waist and the head to indicate the relative degree of highness or lowness of the pitch. Later in the child's musical development the teacher may use the five fingers of the left hand to simulate the musical staff. Various changes in pitch may be designated by pointing, with the other hand, to a certain finger or space between two particular fingers which represents a particular pitch change.

Utilizing bodily motions.   Bodily motions or postures appropriate to the pitch level of the music are another excellent means for further clarifying the concept of tonal direction. The teacher should select an appropriate song, or preferably recorded instrumental music, and prior to listening, ask the children to listen for changing pitch levels. When the pitch becomes higher they may raise their arms, and when the pitch becomes lower they may lower their arms. When appropriate classroom space is available, it is even desirable for the class to interpret the music freely by using their entire bodies in a similar manner. An alternative approach to the use of bodily motions is to have only one student respond while the remainder of the class keep their eyes closed. At an appropriate point in the music, the tone arm of the record player is lifted and the class asked, "Was the music high, medium, or low?" In utilizing songs, the teacher should discuss with the class the relationship between the words and the music of a song, and the fact that certain series of words or sentences often dictate a rise or fall in the musical phrase.

Evaluating and selecting basic song texts

The selection of basic song texts suitable to the teacher's philosophy and to the particular needs of his students is a problem of concern to many persons. To make an intelligent choice one must be guided by certain specific criteria. Following are a set of selected questions which the conscientious teacher must ask himself when considering the selection of basic song texts for grades 1-6.

Songs

1. Are the music and the text of a high quality and in good taste?
2. Do the songs provide a variety of rhythmic as well as tonal experiences?
3. Do the vocal ranges take into consideration the physical development and capabilities of children of differing ages?

4. Does each book contain songs of varying degrees of difficulty?
5. Is there song material suitable for teaching various technical problems appropriate for each grade?
6. Are the words of the songs within the vocabulary of the age group for which the book was designed (or perhaps even a grade lower)?

General content

1. Is a wide selection of folk songs of many countries included in the books?
2. Are songs dealing with a variety of everyday experiences included in the books for younger children?
3. Are art songs by master composers included, particularly in those books designed for intermediate grades?
4. Do the books include some songs relating to various seasons and special holidays?
5. Are the pictures and illustrations related to the music, without detracting from the notation?
6. Does each book provide for review of concepts presented in preceding grades?
7. Is the material presented in such a way as to foster maximum musical growth in each grade level?

Enrichment activities

1. Are an adequate number of songs included that provide for the development of free and patterned rhythmic response?
2. Are suggestions included for creative activity?
3. Are suggestions included for utilizing melody and rhythm instruments?
4. Are chord names included with selected songs to facilitate the playing of autoharp accompaniments?
5. Are a few simple arrangements utilizing band and orchestral instruments included in the books for intermediate grades?

Teacher aids

1. Are suggestions included for correlating recorded music with particular songs?
2. Are suggestions for teaching each song included in the teacher's book?
3. Do the teacher's manuals, or books, provide a well-organized and clearly presented plan for developing musical skills and understandings?
4. Are the recordings of the songs in each book good models of tone, diction, and interpretation?
5. Are piano accompaniments available for the songs and are they easy enough for the average classroom teacher to play?

Format

1. Do the books have a soil-resistant cover, strong binding and durable paper?
2. Is the music notation clear and well-spaced?
3. Is a glossary of tempo and expression markings included in the intermediate grade books?
4. Do the books include both a classified and an alphabetical index?

Topics for discussion

1. Discuss a variety of procedures for presenting a new song to a class. How can the presentation be related to the regular on-going classroom study?

2. What factors influence the teacher's choice of either the whole song or phrase approach to the teaching of a rote song?

3. Since children are likely to imitate the teacher's voice quality, what model should the teacher use?

4. Discuss the relationship between the children's understanding of the words of a song and the rapidity with which they will be able to learn the music.

5. Discuss the variety of types of accompaniment that might be used with songs. On what basis should particular types of accompaniment be chosen?

6. How large a song repertoire should children in different grades have? Should they learn a lot of new songs, or spend most of their time reviewing songs already learned? What factors should influence the teacher's decision?

7. Discuss the problems of the "uncertain singer." What factors are involved in the child's lack of musical development?

8. Describe in detail how the attitudes of a teacher may affect children's development of a positive or negative outlook toward singing.

9. What are some necessary personal attributes of a successful music teacher?

10. What techniques and methods can a teacher use to develop interest and enthusiasm in a child who refuses to sing?

Suggestions for further study

ELLISON, Alfred. *Music with Children*. New York: McGraw-Hill, 1959, Chs. 2 & 3.

JONES, Archie N. *Music Education in Action*. Boston: Allyn and Bacon, 1960, pp. 28-43.

McMILLAN, L. Eileen. *Guiding Children's Growth Through Music*. Boston: Ginn, 1959, Ch. 2.

MURSELL, Manes L. *Music Education: Principles and Programs*. Morristown, N.J.: Silver Burdett, 1956, Ch. 7.

NYE, Robert E. and NYE, Vernice T. *Music in the Elementary School,* 2nd ed. Englewood Cliffs, N.J.: Prentice-Hall, 1964, Ch. 6.

SWANSON, Bessie R. *Music in the Education of Children,* 2nd ed. Belmont, Calif.: Wadsworth, 1964, Chs. 2 & 6.

Suggested materials

BERTAIL, Inez. *Complete Nursery Song Book.* New York: Lothrop, Lee & Shepard, Inc., 1947.

COLEMAN, Jack L., SCHOEPPLE, Irene L., and TEMPLETON, Virginia. *Music for Exceptional Children.* Evanston, Ill.: Summy-Birchard Company, 1964.

CROWNINSHIELD, Ethel. *Mother Goose Songs* (1948). *Sing and Play Book* (1938). *Stories that Sing* (1945). *Songs and Stories About Animals* (1947). *Walk the World Together* (1951). Boston: Boston Music Company.

DAVISON, Archibald T., and SURETTE, Thomas W. *140 Folk-Songs* (Rote Songs for grades I, II, and III). Boston: E. C. Schirmer Music Company, 1944. (Also available with piano accompaniment.)

GLAZER, Tom. *A New Treasury of Folk Songs.* New York: Bantam Books, Inc., 1961.

KAPP, Paul. *A Cat Came Fiddling and Other Rhymes of Childhood.* New York: General Music Publishing Company, Inc., 1956.

KODÁLY, Zoltán, *Fifty Nursery Songs,* [within a range of five notes], London: Boosey & Hawkes, 1962.

LANDECK, Beatrice. *Songs to Grow On* (1950). *More Songs to Grow On* (1954). New York: Edward B. Marks and William Sloan Associates. (Songs recorded by Folkway Records).

NYE, Robert, NYE, Vernice, AUBIN, Neva, and KYME, George. *Singing With Children.* Belmont, Calif.: Wadsworth Publishing Company, 1962.

SEEGER, Ruth C. *American Folk Songs for Children* (1948). *Animal Folk Songs for Children* (1950). *American Folk Songs for Christmas* (1953). Garden City, N.Y.: Doubleday and Company, Inc.

Songs for Every Purpose and Occasion. Minneapolis: Schmitt, Hall & McCreary, 1938.

SNYDER, Alice M. *Sing and Strum.* New York: Mills Music, Inc., 1957.

TOBITT, Janet E. *The Ditty Bag.* Pleasantville, N.Y.: Janet E. Tobitt, 1946.

WOOD, Lucille F., and SCOTT, Louise B. *Singing Fun* (1954). *More Singing Fun* (1961). St. Louis: Webster Publishing Company, 1954. (Songs recorded by Bowmar Records).

All Basic Music Series. For listing of books and publishers, see the Appendix, pp. 252-54.

Films

The Pitch Pipe. (Johnson Hunt Productions, 6509 De Longpre Avenue, Hollywood, Calif.), 1955, b&w, 13 min. Col.

3 Rhythmic activities

~~~~~~

Expressive bodily movement is an integral part of both the music education and the physical education programs. Rhythmic response to music can be a most enjoyable activity that not only improves muscular coordination, but allows for the necessary release of classroom tensions. Through a *study* of rhythm, moreover, music may become more meaningful and a more musical and artistic performance may result. Bodily movement in a creative manner may contribute to the development of an increased awareness and understanding of tempo, dynamics, phrase structure, and mood in music. Rhythmic or bodily response to music develops a feeling for, and an understanding of, pulsation, duration, accent and stress, and provides a necessary and essential background for later experiences in music reading.[1]

Various types of bodily movement suitable for children in the elementary school may be utilized. For purposes of discussion they are categorized into three general types: interpretive or free rhythmic response, patterned responses, and singing games and folk dances. Encompassing both of the first two types is bodily movement, utilized for the purpose of clarifying concepts of musical form.

[1] For a discussion of rhythmic experiences as they relate to music reading, see Chapter 7.

Interpretive response

Interpretive response is essentially creative in nature and may range from very simple movements to the more complete dramatization of a song or instrumental selection. Following are examples of interpretive responses as well as the musical sources from which they may be drawn.

Simple rhythmic movements as an outgrowth of songs

One easily accessible source of music for creative bodily movement is the songs with which a particular group of children are familiar. Various simple movements may develop as a natural outgrowth of studying these songs. For example, after singing a song about a tree (or the wind), the teacher may ask the class to pretend they are a tree that sways from side to side as it is blown about by the wind.[2] The children may stand, stretch their arms upward to simulate the branches of a tree, and then sway from side to side as they imagine they are being blown about in the wind. The teacher should participate also and demonstrate the importance of the stress of the pulsation of the music.

Another example that is more appropriate to the maturity of intermediate grade children is a natural outgrowth of the Chinese Chantey, "Yangtze Boatmen's Chantey" (*Music Near and Far,* Book Four, p. 107, Silver Burdett). Prior to singing the song the teacher should explain that men have sung this song as they drag boats upstream and how the rhythm of the song

[2] For songs suitable for this purpose see "Trees in Autumn," *Music in Our Town,* Book Two (Morristown, N.J.: Silver Burdett, 1956), p. 132; "The Wind," *Birchard Music Series,* Book Two (Chicago: Summy-Birchard, 1962), pp. 98-99; "The Wind," *Singing on Our Way* (Boston: Ginn, 1950), p. 97; "Wind in the Trees," *Singing and Rhyming* (Boston: Ginn, 1950), p. 114.

helped them to pull together and be more effective in their task. After the song has been adequately learned, the teacher may reiterate the above statement and demonstrate "pulling together," leaning forward on the first beat of each measure and back on the third beat, and then ask the class to do likewise as they sing the song. While the preceding two examples illustrate the types of simple bodily movements that are appropriate for different age levels, numerous possibilities exist and will be found by examining the words of songs in the basic text that is available in a particular classroom.

Dramatization of songs

A creative form of bodily movment may be achieved through the dramatization of songs with which the children are familiar. Prior to this activity the children should have had ample experience with the song, including discussion of the meaning of the words. After a reasonable degree of skill and understanding has been achieved, the teacher may either suggest to the children particular actions or movements or, preferably, ask for suggestions from the class as to how the various thoughts in the song might be expressed through pantomime (or "acted out"). Songs with several verses, including slightly different but related thoughts, are the most adaptable for dramatization purposes.

The French folksong, "I Had a Little Sail-boat" (La Bergère) (*140 Folk-Songs,* E. C. Schirmer, p. 30) is, for example, particularly suitable for use with children in the kindergarten or first grade. Approximately a half dozen children may be selected to dramatize the song, while the remainder of the class should provide the descriptive accompaniment by singing the song. In some classes most all of the children will be anxious to participate. In such cases, the teacher should reassure the class and tell them that they will all have an opportunity to participate at another time. The first verse in the song describes a "little sailboat." Appropriate actions might be for a small group of children to form a circle, squat on the floor, stretch their arms upward to simulate the sails on a boat, and then rock slowly from side to side in time to the music. The second verse describes an "ugly frog" that "leaped on her deck." In this verse the children should imagine that they are a frog, assuming appropriate bodily positions and facial expressions. In the third verse, "the ship went topsy-turvy," presumably due to the frog. To depict this, the children should emulate a sinking sailboat, gradually lower their outstretched arms, and "sink" to the floor.

The basic song texts available in each classroom will contain many suitable songs; however, teachers should not limit the many possibilities for such activities to the songs included in any one book. Rather, they should be continually seeking new and suitable materials which may be effectively used for this purpose.

While songs are a good beginning point in dramatization, children will also benefit greatly by dramatizing various types of recorded instrumental music. An excellent source for such recordings is the *RCA Victor Library for Elementary Schools,* Rhythmic Activities, Volumes 1-4. Teachers may tell their class the brief story about the music and, after they have listened to it at least once, select several children to dramatize the actions as the music is played again (the story and dramatization for the music are suggested in the "Notes for Teachers" in the front of each album).

Creative bodily movement as an outgrowth of instrumental music

Instrumental music that suggests certain types of bodily movement may also be effectively utilized with young children. Following are a few examples of activities in which children may participate.

1. "Galloping horses."   Music: "The Wild Horseman" by Robert Schumann (RCA Victor Listening Activities, Volume 2, E78). The children should be asked to listen to the music and see if they can tell the *way* in which the horses are moving. After it has been determined that the music sounds like the horses are "galloping," then four to six children may be selected to "gallop" like horses, preferably in a circle. (A suggested movement is to gallop with one foot always remaining ahead of the other.)

2. "High-stepping horses." Music: "The Happy Farmer" by Robert Schumann (*Album for the Young*, p. 16, G. Schirmer),[3] or "High Stepping Horses" by Anderson (RCA Victor Rhythmic Activities, Volume 1, E71). The same general procedures may be utilized as suggested for "galloping horses." If adequate space for bodily movement is unavailable, the children may quite easily "step" in place, or pretend to be "rocking horses."

3. "Rabbits," "grasshoppers," or " frogs" (or anything that pauses and jumps). Music: "The Grasshoppers" (*Our First Music*, p. 317, C. C. Birchard). The teacher may introduce the music by saying that it describes a rabbit, grasshopper, or frog that sits very still and periodically decides to jump. The children should then be asked to listen carefully to the music and to raise their hands when they feel the "jump" occurs. This is usually quite obvious to kindergarten and first grade children. Several students may then be selected to portray or dramatize the actions while the remainder of the class observes.

4. "Toy soldiers." Music: "March of the Tin Soldiers" by Tschaikovsky (RCA Victor Rhythmic Activities, Volume 3, E73). The teacher may introduce the music by asking the class to listen and decide how they think small toy (or tin) soldiers would march. After a class discussion of this topic, a small group of children may be asked to demonstrate their own particular conceptions of how these soldiers would march.

5. "Indian dances." Children, both boys and girls, enjoy doing Indian dances, which may be an integral part of their work in a unit of study on Indians, generally undertaken in either the second or third grade. As has been previously suggested, a limited number of children should be chosen to dance at one time. It is also suggested that they dance in a circle, simulating

[3] The music may also be found in various intermediate grade piano books. See, for example, *Willis' Roadway to Classics for Piano,* Cincinnati: Willis Music Co., p. 32.

the style of most Indian dances. A variety of recorded selections appropriate for use as an accompaniment may be found in the RCA Victor Album, *Music of the American Indians,* Volume E89. Particularly appropriate, however, is the "Chant of the Eagle Dance," an authentic rendition by the Hopi Indian Chanters.

Teachers may also improvise appropriate music on the piano by playing the eighth note pattern indicated below in the left hand on C# and G#, and any group of the black keys in the right hand.

The above music is simple enough for any teacher to play —even those with very limited musical experience. Children in the second or third grade who have studied piano may also be provided the opportunity to learn this simple accompaniment for dancing. Utilizing one or more drums or tom toms on the rhythmic pattern ♩♩ ♩♩ will add to the total effectiveness of the accompaniment.

6. "Ballet dancing."   Music: "Ballet" by Gluck (RCA Victor Rhythmic Activities, Volume I, E71). Girls especially enjoy imitating the graceful movements of ballet dancers. They may step, turn slowly, whirl, leap, run, or make other appropriate movements. In some classes there may be children who have had lessons in ballet. These students may be asked to demonstrate some simple movements so that the class may develop a general concept of what to do. Whenever possible, those children may give a brief talk about ballet—including the fundamental movements and how they are adapted in an expressive manner to particular types of music. When children with some experience in ballet are unavailable in a particular school, the teacher should precede this type of rhythmic activity by showing an educational film on this topic.[4]

The *RCA Victor Basic Library for Elementary Schools,* Rhythmic Activities, Volumes 1-4, contains many recordings suitable for a variety of other rhythmic activities. Following are some bodily movements appropriate to particular recordings: the jolly antics of clowns, balancing like a tight-rope walker, imitating various animals, dancing like fairies or dwarfs, working at different tasks, and playing various games. These are only a few general examples of innumerable suggestions listed in the "Notes for Teachers" in the front of each album.

Patterned response

The patterned response focuses upon developing an awareness of, and a bodily response to, pulsation, accent and stress in music. Such bodily response to music provides an essential basis for the development of rhythmic security and for later experiences in music reading. Patterned responses are not necessarily noncreative; rather, the emphasis is upon response to pulse and accent in music, instead of free bodily movement. In selecting appropriate activities for children, the teacher should consider the level of the group's bodily maturation. For very young children, movements involving the large bodily muscles should be utilized. As children mature and become better coordinated more intricate movements involving the smaller muscles may be more effectively used. For purposes of discussion, the patterned responses may be placed into various categories.

Walking, running, and skipping

These movements all involve the use of large body muscles and are, therefore, particularly appropriate for use with

4 See, for example, *Ballet Girl*, 23 min., sd., b&w, Brandon Films, Inc., 200 W. 57th Street, New York 19, N.Y., 1956.

kindergarten and first grade children. Prior to the use of actual bodily movements, the class should be asked to listen carefully to a particular musical selection and decide whether walking or running steps would be more appropriate. A small group of children may then be selected to participate. They should be asked to listen to the pulse of the music and try to "step in time" to it. The teacher should then repeat the activity with music of the contrasting tempo and rhythmic movement so that children may develop a greater awareness of the actual differences. Following are some suggested recordings for this purpose, all of which may be located in the *RCA Victor Library for Elementary Schools,* Rhythmic Activities, Volumes 1 and 2.

The University School, Indiana University, and The Daily Herald-Telephone, Bloomington, Ind.

Marching in Kindergarten stimulates response to the pulse of the music.

Walking:

"Wheelbarrow Motive," Volume 1, E71
"Tiptoe March" by Clara L. Anderson, Volume 1, E71
"Air de Ballet" by Jadassohn, Volume 2, E72
"March" by Hollaender (for slow walk, with lunging from side to side) Volume 2, E72

Running:

"Etude Joyeuse" by Kopylow, Volume 1, E71
"Sparks" by Moszkowski, Volume 1, E71
"Running Game" by Gurlett, Volume 2, E72
"L'Arabesque" by Burgmuller, Volume 2, E72

Skipping is a bodily movement that children especially enjoy doing in response to music. Preceding this activity, music suitable for the purpose should be played and the children asked to guess the type of bodily movement they feel might be appropriate. With most children, the desired movement is rather easily identified. The class may be further led into a discussion of why they often skip during play and how they feel when they skip. Several children may then be selected for the skipping activity or, when adequate space is available, a larger portion of the class may be allowed to participate. Following are several suggested recordings, also in the *RCA Victor Library for Elementary Schools,* that are appropriate for this activity.

"Skipping Theme" by Clara L. Anderson, Volume 1, E71
"Theme for Skipping," Volume 1, E71
"Plain Skip," Volume 1, E71
"Gigue in A" by Corelli, Volume 2, E72

In addition to simple skipping as a bodily response, variations of this activity may be also utilized with the above-mentioned recordings. Kindergarten and first grade children especially enjoy the musical game, "Skip and Stoop," which involves simply the group skipping while the music is being played and stopping and stooping when the music stops, *i.e.,* when the teacher lifts the arm of the phonograph. When the music resumes, the children begin again to skip. In a way, this game or activity is similar to "musical chairs," except that in the former game, children are not eliminated from the game at any point. It is strongly recommended that any competitive aspects of the game be avoided when used with this particular age group, as children of this age have not matured sufficiently to be "eliminated" or to lose in such an activity. Let the entire class be "winners."

Skipping rope in time to the music is an activity that is especially enjoyed by girls in the second grade. Most are able to execute this activity quite well. However, all should be advised to listen to the beat or pulse of the music and to skip in time to the music. Boys, while not particularly adept at skipping rope, nor desirous of learning, often enjoy bouncing a large rubber ball (about the size of a soccer ball) in time to the music. Prior to undertaking this activity the boys should be instructed to use *both* hands and to bounce the ball somewhat easily. It is often helpful to practice bouncing the ball for awhile before adapting the movements to music.

It may be found that some children in a given class are somewhat uncoordinated and unable to walk, run, or skip in time to the tempo of a particular recorded selection. It is generally felt that most all children can learn to move in time to music—but sometimes only at their own speed, one in which their bodily movements are most coordinated. It would be well for the teacher, in assisting such children, to observe carefully their rate of movement and to then adapt the tempo of the music to the children's abilities. To do this, however, the teacher must play the music on some instrument, such as the piano, in which the tempo may be adjusted to the children's capabilities.

Classroom teachers may learn to improvise on the piano their own music for walking, running, and skipping. First, they should understand and practice the basic I, IV, V⁷, I chord progression.

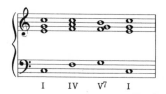

These chords may be played in a tempo and in combinations appropriate for walking, running, or skipping. For walking, the teacher might play:

For running, the teacher may use the same pattern in the right hand, but simply play eighth notes in the left hand:

For skipping, the same basic chord progression may also be used, but the meter should be changed to 6/8 and the rhythmic pattern altered:

After learning these basic patterns, the teacher will undoubtedly wish to improvise others that allow for greater rhythmic and tonal variety. In addition, the classroom teacher will want to either explore and study composed music written expressly for this purpose [5] or to adapt music in various piano books to his needs.

5 See Robert Pace, *Piano for Classroom Music*, Englewood Cliffs, N.J.: Prentice-Hall, Inc., 1956.

Rapping, tapping, and clapping

The simple muscular responses of rapping, tapping, and clapping are particularly suitable for facilitating the children's response to the pulsation of the music. These activities are generally most useful when used in connection with the study of a particular song as a means of developing greater awareness of, and improved bodily response to, the pulse or beat. Each of the three responses have a particular value in terms of providing variety to the activity and should be periodically alternated. Each, of course, involves a different dynamic level because of the nature of the response. The choice of a particular one will depend upon the nature and the mood of the music. For a response of a medium dynamic level, rapping is suggested. Each student may be asked to listen for the pulse of the music and to respond by rapping his knuckles upon his desk. For music necessitating a softer response, the students may be asked to tap on their desks with the tips of their fingers or with the end of their pencils. For example, in utilizing such a response with the song, "The Shoemaker" (*Music in our Town,* p. 75, Book Two, Silver Burdett), each student may be asked to imagine he is driving small nails in the sole of his shoe. If the music is a more vigorous nature, such as, for example, "Do Lord, Remember Me" (American folk-song) [6] then the clapping in response to the pulsation of the music may be more appropriate.

In addition to responding to the pulse of the music, students may rap, tap, or clap the rhythm of a song. This helps them to feel the precise rhythmic duration of the various patterns. A further device to develop awareness of rhythmic patterns is for the teacher to clap, or tap out, the rhythms of various songs and ask the class to identify the title of each. An alternative to this procedure would be for the teacher to write on the chalkboard the rhythmic patterns of various songs (usually the first phrase is sufficient) and see if the class can identify them. For example, can you identify the tune that is set in this rhythm? [7]

6 See *Birchard Music Series, Book Three,* Evanston, Ill.: Summy-Birchard, 1962, p. 92.

7 The answer is "Dixie."

Marking activities

Marking activities are simply a response to pulse and accent through marking on the chalkboard or a sheet of paper at one's desk. They are appropriate to the maturity of children in the intermediate grades. In addition to developing a precise physical response to the pulse, an increased awareness of stress or accent also occurs through visual portrayal. That is, a slightly larger mark may be used for accented than for unaccented beats. A 2/4 march may, for example, elicit this type of response on the chalkboard:

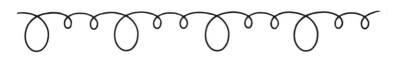

A waltz, or other music in moderate triple meter, might be expressed as follows:

Marking activities may often be adapted to current units of study by devising or creating symbols or simple line drawings that relate to the topic at hand, but which still offer opportunity for the student to respond to pulse and accent in the music. For example, in the fall of the year, the following simple drawing—for quadruple meter—might be appropriate for Halloween:

Or, for triple meter, the students might simulate wheat shocks at harvest time:

Or, perhaps during the spring of the year, the class may utilize markings that simulate trees:

The preceding are given as examples only, and the imaginative teacher will most likely be able to devise many other marking activities appropriate to current topics of study.

Conducting

Students in the intermediate grades may benefit from learning the basic conducting patterns and utilizing them in response to the pulse of the music. In some instances, the entire class may conduct a particular song. At other times, the teacher may select one particular student and ask him to come to the front of the room to conduct the class in the singing of a song. The objective of such a procedure is, of course, not necessarily to make "conductors" of the entire class, but simply to provide another means through which they may respond to the pulse and accent in music. This does not mean to imply that the basic conducting movements be taken lightly; rather, each student should learn to conduct as well as possible, within the range or limits of his capabilities. The more adept the students are the more the teacher may expect of them. Following are the basic conducting patterns for duple, triple, quadruple, and sextuple meter.[8]

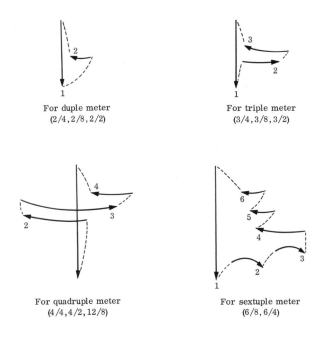

For duple meter
(2/4, 2/8, 2/2)

For triple meter
(3/4, 3/8, 3/2)

For quadruple meter
(4/4, 4/2, 12/8)

For sextuple meter
(6/8, 6/4)

Singing games and folk dances

Singing games and folk dances may contribute to children's musical development in that they dramatize and

[8] For more detailed information on conducting techniques, see Robert L. Garretson, *Conducting Choral Music,* 2nd ed. Boston: Allyn and Bacon, Inc., 1965, Chapter 2.

lend meaning to the text of a song. Some students who, for example, have not found their singing voices may be drawn to
music through this type of activity. In addition, this activity
contributes to the development of bodily coordination and is
another desirable means of releasing classroom tensions that
build up during the day. Singing games are appropriate to the
objectives of both the primary and intermediate grades, while
folk dances are utilized primarily in intermediate grades.

Before teaching the movements to a singing game the teacher
should make sure that the class knows the song well, so that
they will be able to better concentrate their attention upon the
movements. Whenever feasible it is desirable to move the students from the classroom to some larger area, such as the school
gymnasium, so that they won't be hampered in their movements.
When this is possible the entire class may participate in the
activity. In schools where such is not available, and the activities
must be held within the confines of the classroom, then other
approaches must be used. For some of the singing games involving simpler movements (such as "Looby Loo"), the class may
participate in the aisles between the seats. If this procedure is
unfeasible then it becomes necessary that only part of the class
participate in the rhythmic activity, while the remainder of the
group sings the song. This approach is sometimes justified any-
way because it is not easy to concentrate on certain rhythmic
movements while singing. In classrooms where limited space is
available many difficulties can arise when too many students endeavor to participate at one time. A good procedure is for the
class to "take turns" in doing the various activities.

It is generally best for the teacher to demonstrate the games
or dances and lead the class through the routine. This approach
is much more preferable than only a verbal explanation, which
is often relatively meaningless. In this case, a demonstration is
worth much more than any well-chosen words.

A variety of singing games may be found in the basic music
series. Directions for these songs may usually be found at the
bottom of the page, or in the teacher's manual. Other sources include record albums of selected singing games and folk dances.
The album, *Singing Games,* is particularly recommended for

Cincinnati Public Schools

Folk games necessitate that children listen carefully to the rhythm of the music.

use with children in the primary grades.[9] The directions for each of the twenty-one singing games included are explained and/or diagrammed in a brochure that accompanies the album. Among the titles are such favorites as "Did You Ever See a Lassie?" "Here We Go 'Round the Mulberry Bush," "Looby Loo," "The Muffin Man," "Ten Little Indians," "Way Down in the Paw Paw Patch," "Yankee Doodle," and many others.

Folk dances may also make a valuable contribution to intermediate grade children. They are generally, however, more complicated and involved than singing games. Therefore, classroom teachers and music specialists should not attempt the introduction of such activities without adequate knowledge and experience with the dances and an understanding of the best ways of presenting them.[10] In this phase of school activities

[9] RCA Victor Record Library for Elementary Schools, *Singing Games for Primary Grades,* Album E87.

[10] For a square dance record series, ranging in difficulty from album to album, see *Let's Square Dance,* edited and recorded by Richard Krause, RCA Victor (5 albums), available at 33⅓, 45, and 78 r.p.m. Each album includes illustrated instructions.

teachers would do well to consult and cooperate with the physical education specialist, who generally has had specialized training in this area.

Classroom teachers may wish to include folk dances as a part of the study of a particular unit or topic. They frequently are utilized as a part of the culminating portion of a unit, perhaps presented as an assembly program for the school. In such cases, the physical education instructor may teach the dances, with the classroom teacher assuming the responsibility of arranging for appropriate costumes and relating the cultural aspects of the dance to the unit being studied.[11]

Teaching concepts of form through bodily movement

As children develop facility in reading they soon learn that a sentence is a group of words expressing a thought or an idea. Children should also be helped to find musical sentences or phrases in the songs they are singing. This will be comparatively easy because the phrases in many of the songs in the basic series are written on separate staves. Of course, this doesn't occur with all songs. Therefore, other means of identifying phrases should also be used. Children may find cues by examining the text of the song and looking for commas and periods. More important, however, is for children to develop an awareness of the rise and fall, or melodic contour of phrases. Also, after examining carefully the first phrase of a song, the class should scan the song and look for phrases that are identical, similar, or different.

Children's understanding of phrases, while vague and hazy at the outset, may also be clarified through appropriate bodily movement. For example, to indicate the rise and fall of the phrase they may slowly raise and lower their arms, move the arms in a

11 See Ruth L. Murray, *Dance in Elementary Education*, New York: Harper, 1953, Chapters 9-12.

slow circular motion, or they may move their right arm from left to right in a curved pattern. If the tempo of a song is moderate they may walk in time to it and reverse directions at the beginning of each new phrase.[12]

As children's understanding of phrases is clarified through the procedures mentioned above they will gain a concept of unity and variety as an essential of musical form. The ternary

Cincinnati Public Schools

Arm movement is one method for clarifying and checking children's comprehension of phrasing.

[12] Another related procedure of teaching understanding of phrases is simply to divide the class into two groups and have them alternately sing each phrase. Still another means is through the playing of different groups of rhythm instruments on each phrase. For a discussion of these procedures, see Chapter 5.

form A B A, for example, will take on greater meaning.[13] Bodily movement may also be utilized to clarify the concept of ternary form in the more extended musical works. Again, if the tempo is moderate they may walk in time to the music and reverse directions when the contrasting musical material is introduced. During the reiteration of the first section, they may again reverse directions. Some selections written in ternary form are more obvious than others because of a distinct change in mood and/or tempi. For this reason, the selection, "Run, Run" from *Memories of Childhood* by Octavio Pinto (*RCA Victor Listening Activities,* Volume 1, E77) is particularly recommended for the initial use of this approach. In this selection the tempo of the first and last parts would necessitate a quick running movement, while the middle section would demand a slow walk.

Opportunity should also be allowed for more creative bodily movement that depicts the mood of the music. For example, in the Chopin *Prelude No. 15* ("The Raindrop"), the children might move gracefully and lightly to the first and last sections and in a stalking manner on the somewhat sombre middle section. After listening to particular musical selections children should discuss various possible movements and then select those that they feel are most appropriate. Through the making of considered choices and then evaluating their effectiveness, children are allowed further opportunities for musical growth.

Topics for discussion

1.   Describe the differences between creative rhythmic response and patterned response. What is the specific contribution of each to the musical education of children?

2.   What specific concepts of music can be learned through participation in rhythmic activities?

[13] See Chapter 4 for related listening experiences.

3. Discuss the importance of establishing a feeling for pulse in elementary school children.

4. Discuss the importance of proper motivation in the presentation of rhythmic activities.

5. Discuss a variety of types of musical accompaniment that may be used for rhythmic activities. In what type of activity would each be most appropriate?

6. How can the classroom teacher encourage the awkward or uncoordinated child to enjoy and participate in rhythmic activities?

Suggestions for further study

ANDREWS, Gladys. *Creative Rhythmic Movement for Children.* Englewood Cliffs, N.J.: Prentice-Hall, 1954.

CLEMENS, James R. *Invitation to Rhythm.* Dubuque, Iowa: Wm. C. Brown Company, Publishers, 1962.

DRIVER, Ann. *Music and Movement.* London: Oxford, 1947.

ELLISON, Alfred. *Music With Children.* New York: McGraw-Hill, 1959, Ch. 4.

HOOD, Marguerite V. and SCHULTZ, E. J. *Learning Music Through Rhythm.* Boston: Ginn, 1949.

HUGHES, Dorothy. *Rhythmic Games and Dances.* New York: American Book, 1942.

HUMPHREYS, Louise and ROSS, Jerrold. *Interpreting Music Through Movement.* Englewood Cliffs, N.J.: Prentice-Hall, 1964.

KRAUS, Richard. *Play Activities for Boys and Girls.* New York: McGraw-Hill, 1957, Chs. 7 & 8.

MURRAY, Ruth L. *Dance in Elementary Education.* New York: Harper & Row, 1953.

MURSELL, James L. *Music Education: Principles and Programs.* Morristown, N.J.: Silver Burdett, 1956, Ch. 9.

PIERCE, Anne E. *Teaching Music in the Elementary School*. New York: Holt, Rinehart and Winston, 1959, Ch. 6.

SHEEHY, Emma D. *Children Discover Music and Dance*. New York: Holt, Rinehart and Winston, 1959, Chs. 7 & 12.

Suggested materials

ANDREWS, Gladys. *Creative Rhythmic Movement for Children*. Englewood Cliffs, N.J.: Prentice-Hall, Inc., 1954.

DOLL, Edna, and NELSON, Mary Jarman. *Rhythms Today*. Morristown, N.J.: Silver Burdett Company, 1965.

GERI, Frank H. *Illustrated Games and Rhythms for Children: Primary Grades*. Englewood Cliffs, N.J.: Prentice-Hall, Inc., 1955.

HAMLIN, Alice P., and GUESSFORD, Margaret G. *Singing Games for Children*. Cincinnati: The Willis Music Company, 1941.

LA SALLE, Dorothy. *Rhythms and Dances for Elementary Schools*, Revised Edition. New York: A. S. Barnes & Company, 1951.

LATCHAW, Marjorie, and PYATT, Jean. *A Pocket Guide of Dance Activities*. Englewood Cliffs, N.J.: Prentice-Hall, Inc., 1958.

SAFFRAN, Rosanna B. *First Book of Creative Rhythms*. New York: Holt, Rinehart and Winston, Inc., 1963.

SEATTER, Elizabeth, MINNIS, Enola, and WALLACE, Annabel S. *Romp In Rhythm*. Cincinnati: The Willis Music Company, 1944.

Skip to My Lou, 17 Singing Games. New York: Girl Scouts of the United States of America.

TOBITT, Janet E. *Promenade All: A Compilation of Song-Dances*. Pleasantville, N.Y.: Janet E. Tobitt, 1947.

WEILAND, Adell Marie. *Music, Rhythms, and Games*. Chicago: Follett Publishing Company, 1953.

WILSON, Harry R., and HUNT, Beatrice A. *Sing and Dance*. Minneapolis: Schmitt, Hall & McCreary Company, 1945.

Films

Building Children's Personalities With Creative Dancing (University of California, Univ. Extension, Education Film Sales Dept., Los Angeles, Calif.), Film No. 5844, Col.

Rhythm Is Everywhere (Carl F. Mahnke Productions, 215 E. 3rd St., Des Moines, Iowa), 1946, b&w, 11 min., Elem.

Rhythm Instruments and Movements (Encyclopaedia Britannica Films, 1150 Wilmette Ave., Wilmette, Ill.), 1950, b&w, 11 min., Elem./Col.

4 Experiences in listening

Listening is involved in all avenues of musical activity, whether it be singing, rhythmic activities or expressive bodily movement, playing instruments, or in creative activities. In singing, students must listen carefully to themselves and to each other as well as to the musical accompaniment. Rhythmic activity involves careful listening to the pulse and/or the rhythm of the music, as well as to the mood and form which often suggests types of expressive bodily movement. In the playing of instruments, the child must again listen carefully to both his own playing and that of others. Successful creative activities involve the child's awareness of his own creative efforts, as well as that of others, and ultimately an evaluation of his own work if improvement is to occur. Listening of some type is involved in all music activities.

In addition to listening in the ways described above, children will find their musical world enhanced if they learn *how* to listen to the music performed by others. Intelligent listening involves certain basic knowledge. Ways of helping children to develop skill in the application of this knowledge to the music they hear is the primary concern of this chapter.

The importance of listening

Music is an integral part of our culture and one cannot live in today's modern society without being exposed to a considerable amount of music. Music is all about us. It has its function as a part of religious worship, in official governmental and Armed Forces ceremonies, at national political conventions, in the home and the school. It serves to heighten the dramatic effects in motion pictures and television productions. It is a requisite to social dancing, as well as to more serious modern dance and ballet. Most important, however, is the pleasure and satisfaction derived from listening to music as a serious art form. Concerts by the major symphony orchestras and professional choirs, programs on radio and television, as well as the vast amount of recorded music available today provide ample opportunity for the public, if it wishes, to benefit from music's lasting values.

Often music is used simply as a background, *e.g.,* incidental music for parties and in shopping centers. Music is also effectively used to help children relax during rest periods, and as "company" while one studies or does his homework. All these sounds occurring about us do not always register because of our preoccupation with other matters. This is understandable and sometimes even necessary. The fact that music "soothes" is also understandable and desirable to a certain extent. But music can make a very tangible contribution to a person's life, and to do so it must be raised from the level of merely "background" music. It is unfortunate whenever children consider music as something only incidental to other seemingly more important activities. To be fully appreciated music must be studied and understood. Only in this way will it assume its proper place in the child's life.

From the musical skills and understandings developed in the public schools, many children derive benefit by continuing their participation in such activities throughout life. The great majority of students, however, will ultimately join the vast army of consumers of music, in that while they do not actively participate, many will become quite active listeners and often the principal supporters of musical organizations in their community. This support will occur primarily through attendance at various programs and concerts and through the purchase of recordings. It is upon this segment of the American people that the future growth of music in America depends. Therefore, our schools need to adequately prepare our future citizens for this eventuality. Therein is the basis for the justification of the general music classes in our schools. The teacher's task is to teach boys and girls *what* to listen for, *how* to listen, and finally *when* to listen. This is essential to raising the musical tastes of the American public.

Developing appreciation

The matter of developing appreciation has been much discussed in recent years by music educators and others concerned with improving the musical tastes of the public. Webster defines *appreciate* as "to recognize or feel the worth of." In other words, appreciation involves both the knowing and feeling of something. Genuine appreciation involves both an intellectual and an emotional response. Many years ago, some persons endeavored to refute this argument by saying that you didn't have to understand the beauties of a sunset to appreciate it—you simply had to sit back, bask in its beauties, and enjoy it. While such an argument may have some validity in regard to sunsets, it does not apply to music and is really off the point. It has not been heard for some time. Emotional and intellectual response really go hand in hand, each contributing to the other. In listening to music, a person should respond emotionally—he should be aware of how it makes him feel, how it influences his behavior. Emotional response should and often does stimulate a desire to learn more about music itself—it should lead one on to a further exploration of the world of sound. Intellectual response, on the other hand, may come about in a variety of ways. A listener may be intrigued by a certain composition simply because of the knowledge he may have about a particular combination of instruments or voices, or perhaps by some bit of knowledge about the composer or the composer's intent in writing the music. This knowledge or interest often does and should lead a person to a greater enjoyment of music and a greater emotional response.

Of course, it has been said that some persons know very

little about music and simply enjoy "basking" in it, while other persons listen to music in a calculating, somewhat analytical manner. No two people can be expected to listen in exactly the same way. However, most persons would agree that maximum appreciation or enjoyment occurs when there is some degree of balance between emotional and intellectual involvement. Therefore, one of the objectives of our school listening program should be the planning of an instructional program which furthers the development of both these aspects in the listening habits of school youth.

Learning to listen

Habits of intelligent and insightful listening do not occur automatically; they must be carefully developed. It has been said that the principal objective of the listening program in the kindergarten-primary grades is to teach children to "learn to listen," while in the intermediate grades children should "listen to learn." This is perhaps a gross over-simplification of the listening objectives; we desire that children in the kindergarten-primary grades learn something definite from their listening lessons, and in the intermediate grades we continually endeavor to teach toward improved habits and increased skills in listening. The preceding statement does, however, point up the teacher's initial concern or problem—that of teaching boys and girls correct habits of listening and how to be most receptive to the worthwhile music which they do hear about them in everyday life. In addition, boys and girls in the intermediate grades have become considerably more mature and capable of hearing and understanding more detail and greater complexities in the music they hear.

Topics for stimulating interest

Following are several areas for listening lessons, as well as for stimulating interest and motivating kindergarten-primary children toward the development of improved listening habits.

Exploring sounds in everyday life.   A good beginning point in the development of listening skills is for the classroom teacher to help children in kindergarten and first grade explore some of the sounds that exist in everyday life. The children should discuss these various sounds, endeavor to describe their similarities and differences with other sounds, and try to imitate them. They should then be led into a discussion of the changes of pitch and rhythm involved in each particular sound. Whereas pitch changes will often be described by children only in reference to "up and down," various rhythmic patterns may be chanted or even "tapped out" on the desk. Following are some of the many topics which may thus be explored: the wail of fire sirens, the sound of various types of bells (church bells, school bells, cowbells, doorbells, etc.), the howl of the wind, the sound of different automobile horns, the chant of the newsboy, the singing of birds, the patter of the rain, a singing teakettle, the "tick-tock" of large and small clocks, the rustle of leaves, the roll of thunder, the sound of footsteps, the sound of engines (automobile, steam and diesel train engines, and conventional and jet airplane engines), and various animal sounds.[1]

Musical stories.   There are numerous stories of considerable interest to young children that are now available on records. Music is a very integral part of the musical story, with much of the story being told or related through song. One may thus differentiate between the musical story and the story in which music is utilized only as a background to heighten the dramatic effect of the narration. While the musical story is felt to be more advantageous to the purposes of the music teacher, both types have certain values—principally in helping young children to focus their attention upon a "listening" record. In using such

---

[1] As a later activity, students might listen to short selections of music which use these sounds as integral components of composition, especially Edgar Varèse's "Dèserts," which uses dynamically some of the sounds mentioned in this discussion.

materials, the teacher should first present a brief overview of the contents of the story and then ask the children to listen for and be prepared to tell him, after listening to the record, the names of the principal characters, what they did, and perhaps some of the things they said. Through this procedure the teacher learns not only the children's reactions to the record, but the extent to which they understand the story. In addition, by "drawing out" the children in this manner, a helpful summary of the group's experience is provided. In many cases it will be desirable to play the record again on subsequent days. Utilizing similar discussions, as previously suggested, will help to provide further insight and understanding into the content and meaning of the story.

Since the attention span of young children is relatively short, the teacher should avoid playing lengthy recordings all in one sitting. It is better in such cases to divide the recording into portions of suitable length and present them on successive days. It is usually best for the teacher to base his judgments principally on the maturity and background of the particular group of students. In general, listening lessons for younger children should not exceed from four to six minutes, but the length may be modified at the discretion of the teacher. Following are some exceptionally popular musical stories, which the teacher may well consider for use with his students.

> "Pinnochio" (Children's Record Guild, 208)—grades 1-4.
> "Rusty in Orchestraville" (Capitol, L-3007)—grades 1-4.
> "Peter and the Wolf" by Serge Prokofiev (Columbia, ML-4038)—grades 1-6.
> "Peer Gynt and the Trolls" by Edvard Grieg (Musicraft, M-77)—grades 1-6.
> "Cinderella" by Serge Prokofiev (Children's Record Guild, 201)—grades 1-4.
> "Tubby the Tuba" (Decca, CU-106)—grades 1-6.

Music on topics of immediate interest. Another means of stimulating interest is to select music which is of immediate interest to children. Music which holds particular appeal for children of an early age includes such topics as animals, birds,

Cincinnati Public Schools

Displays relating to children's listening topics provide interest and may clarify learning concepts.

toys, other children, gnomes, dwarfs and fairies, and so on.[2] Some suggested titles are as follows:

> "March of the Little Lead Soldiers" by Pierné (RCA Victor Listening Activities, Volume 1, E77)
>
> "Dwarfs" by Reinhold (RCA Victor Rhythm Activities, Volume 1, E71)

---

2 For a variety of topics and highly suitable listening material for children, see the RCA Victor Basic Listening Program, Volumes 1-6.

"Gnomes" by Reinhold (RCA Victor Rhythm Activities, Volume 1, E71)

"Hobby Horse" by Pinto (RCA Victor Rhythm Activities, Volume 1, E71)

"The Wild Horseman" by Schumann (RCA Victor Listening Activities, Volume 2, E78)

"Train to the Zoo" (Children's Record Guild, 1001)

"Four Bears" (Children's Record Guild, 1009)

"The Merry Toy Shop" (Children's Record Guild, 1022)

Records on the preceding general topics will often hold more interest for children if correlated with the other classroom work, specifically with the study unit which the children are currently exploring. Listening lessons which grow out of, and are an integral part of, the study of a unit are generally more meaningful to the students; motivation is high and less time may be necessary for preparing the students to listen, thus leaving more time for actual listening activities.

The attitude of the teacher

The attitude of the teacher can have either a positive or a negative effect upon the development of good listening habits in children. Teachers should give thoughtful consideration to this important matter.

Above all, the teacher should *look interested!* This is especially important, since many children look to the teacher for guidance and direction. While some children may simply mimic the teacher, others will strongly identify with him, thus unconsciously assuming certain of his attitudes and traits.

During the listening lesson, the teacher should assume a position generally somewhere near the record player (in the event the volume needs to be adjusted or the record changed), and assume an attitude of thoughtful attention. He should avoid wandering around the room, adjusting window shades or opening windows, etc. While these things are important, they are nevertheless distracting and should be attended to prior to the listening session.

In general, the teacher should avoid talking during the playing of the record. Explanatory remarks should be made prior to playing the record. However often it may seem desirable to verbally point out certain things about the music, the practice can usually be avoided by careful planning and appropriate explanation prior to the actual listening. If remarks are deemed necessary they should certainly be kept to a minimum. Again, talking can be disconcerting to the children and often the supposed values of the teacher's remarks are offset by the children missing important portions of the record.

The teacher should endeavor to create in the children a "listening mood." By his tone of voice and appropriate facial expressions, he can create a feeling or sense of anticipation—essential to maximum enjoyment and concentration of the listener's attention. Certainly any problems in this area will be minimized if the teacher actually enjoys music himself and is eager to use it as a means of enriching the children's lives.

Guided listening

Students are likely to gain increased insight and understanding of music only to the extent that they are able to concentrate upon certain aspects of it. Unfortunately, without teacher guidance children are not likely to do so. By their very nature they are likely to become restless, their attention is apt to wander, and they may resort to a multitude of types of "out-of-field" behavior, which are generally indicative of a lack of appropriate teacher guidance. Teachers should employ what is commonly referred to as "guided listening." This simply means that the teacher asks the students to listen for something specific during the playing of the record, with the understanding that they will be questioned about it later. This procedure helps to focus the children's attention upon certain specifics; such focus is essential if increased insight and understanding of music is to occur. In addition, it "occupies" the children and lessens the temptations toward "out-of-field" behavior. Highly important, moreover, is that guided listening sets the stage for a more serious and thoughtful approach to the listening of music and dispels any ideas on the children's part that music is simply sound by which they are to be entertained.

General procedures

In utilizing guided listening, the teacher should employ the three-step procedure of *preparation, presentation,* and *follow-up.* The teacher will adequately prepare the children for what they are to hear by providing them with a general and brief over-view, and then by asking them to listen for or to some specific aspect of the music. Advice, such as, "The more carefully you listen, the more you hear!" is recommended. Next, the teacher should play the recording, paying particular attention to the volume adjustment of the record player, and endeavoring to avoid unnecessary comments during the actual listening session. Then, following the playing of the recording, the teacher should question and discuss with the children what they have heard and their impressions and feelings about it.[3] Only through this procedure will the children gain the utmost benefit from the listening sessions.

Topics for lessons in guided listening

Of the many available topics that may be used for listening lessons the following are suggested because of the concrete learning experiences they provide. Some are suitable only for children in kindergarten and first grade. Others, because of their more intricate nature, are suitable only when the children have reached a greater degree of maturity, and should be used only in the fifth or sixth grades. (Following each topic, the sug-

[3] This same general three-step procedure of *preparation, presentation,* and *follow-up* should also be utilized with other types of visual aids, including motion picture films, slides, film-strips; special illustrative materials, such as maps, charts and drawings; and even with field trips to important locations in the community.

gested grade level for which the topic is considered appropriate is usually given.) Some of the initial topics will be found suitable for only a limited time, while others may be used over a period of time until, in the teacher's judgement, the students demonstrate a satisfactory degree of understanding. Although the topics are basic, variety may be provided by using different music. First, the students will develop a general awareness of these musical "problems," then increased insight will gradually occur, and finally a reasonable degree of understanding will be reached.

The following topics are not meant to be an exhaustive list of approaches to listening lessons. They are merely suggested basic approaches to the guided listening program which also may be supplemented by other topics which the teacher feels are appropriate for his particular class.

Tempo.   The initial study of tempo is appropriate even for children in the first grade. The teacher should simply ask the class to listen and decide if the music seems fast or slow. An even simpler approach would be to ask the children if the tempo of the music sounds fast, as in running, or slower as in walking. Comparing the initial listening experiences in tempo to running or walking provides the child with a more concrete basis for making a judgment. While such knowledge seems quite elementary to the experienced musician, it is not always so with a young child, and a reasonable number of listening lessons on this topic will provide the child with a basis for the making of more subtle judgments about tempo during subsequent listening lessons. Some suggested recordings for use with this topic are as follows:

> "Run Run" (first section) from *Memories of Childhood* by Octavio Pinto (RCA Victor Listening Activities, Volume 1, E77)
>
> "Run, Run, Run" by Concone (RCA Victor Rhythmic Activities, Volume 2, E72)
>
> "Andantino" (from *Raymond* Overture) by Thomas (RCA Victor Listening Activities, Volume 2, E78)
>
> "Northern Song" by Robert Schumann (RCA Victor Rhythmic Activities, Volume 3, E73)

Young children should also learn to identify gradual changes in tempo—either faster or slower (*accelerando* and *ritardando*). The teacher should begin by asking the children to "listen carefully and decide if the music gets gradually faster or gradually slower." These tempo changes may be compared to the gradual speeding up of a merry-go-round and the gradual slowing down at the end of the ride. Using the piano or some other instrument to illustrate changing tempi is preferable to recordings, as the initial experience should be made somewhat obvious to young children if they are to comprehend the concept. In most cases the changes in recorded music are likely to be somewhat subtle. Once the children fully understand the concept, however, a variety of recorded music may be utilized. The "Acceleration Waltz" by Strauss is a good beginning point. The slight *ritardandos* at the ends of certain selections also provide desirable focal points for listening lessons. A most interesting example, containing *accelerando* and *ritardando,* as well as many abrupt changes in tempi, is the Brahms *Hungarian Dances*.

Dynamics.   For the initial lessons on this topic, the teacher should simply ask the children to listen carefully and decide if the music sounds "loud" or "soft." This question is made more meaningful if dynamics are compared to "loud as in shouting," and "soft as in a whisper." Examples of recorded music appropriate for children in the first and second grades are as follows:

> Excerpt from "Light Cavalry Overture" by Von Suppe (RCA Victor Listening Activities, Volume 2, E78)
> "March—Trumpet and Drum" (from *Petite Suite*) by Georges Bizet (RCA Victor Listening Activities, Volume 1, E77)
> "Lullaby" by Wolfgang Amadeus Mozart (RCA Victor Listening Activities, Volume 1, E77)
> "Cradle Song" by Franz Schubert (RCA Victor Listening Activities, Volume 1, E77)

Once the basis for understanding the extreme contrasts in dynamics has been provided, the more subtle gradations in dynamics may be discussed. The complete range of dynamics from *ppp* to *fff* may be illustrated on the chalkboard, and after appropriate preliminary experiences, children in the intermediate grades may be asked to listen for some of the more subtle dynamic changes in certain selected recordings. Gradual changes in dynamics (*crescendo* and *descrescendo*) may also serve as focal points for listening lessons. An excellent example illustrating gradual *crescendo* and *decrescendo* is "Norwegian Rustic March" from *Lyric Suite* by Edvard Grieg (*Adventures in Music,* Grade 4, Volume 1, RCA Victor). A composition illustrating the use of a gradual *crescendo,* from the beginning to the climax of the music, is "Bolero" by Maurice Ravel.

Mood.   The study of mood in music is a topic that has un-limited possibilities for listening lessons for all grades in elementary school. Almost any music which portrays a particular mood may be used. The following are examples appropriate for use with young children.

> "Scherzo" from Symphony No. 3 by Beethoven (RCA Victor Listening Activities, Volume 1, E77)
> "Dwarfs" by Reinhold (RCA Victor Rhythmic Activities, Volume 1, E71)
> "Minuet" by Ignace Paderewski (RCA Victor Listening Activities, Volume 1, E77)

For children in the first and second grades, questions pertaining to mood should be structured rather simply, depending of course upon the nature of the music being used. For example, prior to playing the "Scherzo" by Beethoven, the teacher may simply ask, "Listen to the music and decide if it sounds gay and happy or sad and gloomy." At early stages of their growth in learning to listen, this type of guidance is appropriate. As children become more experienced in listening to music, they will be able to volunteer their own comments. Before playing the "Dwarfs" by Reinhold, the teacher might ask, "Does the music sound slow and scary or fast and happy?" Children may also be asked to listen for certain characteristics of the music. For example, the question may be asked about the "Minuet" by

Paderewski, "Does the music sound light and graceful, or heavy and awkward?"

For children in the second and third grades, the question may be "Does the mood, or the tempo, change in one part of the music?" Since tempo and mood are closely related, it is often desirable to point out this relationship to the children and ask them to listen for changes in both. "Run Run" from *Memories of Childhood* by Octavio Pinto (RCA Victor Listening Activities, Volume 1, E77) is an example of music suggested for use with this approach.

For children in the intermediate grades, still another approach to the study of mood may be utilized. The teacher may write on the chalkboard a list of descriptive words and, before playing the recording, ask the class to listen carefully and identify the words that they feel most accurately describe the mood of the music. Following is a suggested list that may be used as a beginning point in the selection of words particularly appropriate, both to the music being studied and to the vocabulary level of the children being taught.[4]

tranquil, quiet	wild, savage
dignified	weird
stately	exotic, strange
majestic	colorful
triumphant	melancholy, sad
lively	sombre, gloomy
cheerful	eerie, weird
bombastic	mysterious
furious	threatening

After the presentation of the music, the teacher should discuss the mood of the music with the students and determine the extent to which agreement occurs among the class. Since mood is not always an absolute factor, and is more a personal experience with each student, the teacher should avoid giving the impression that there is only one answer. Students should be

[4] For a discussion of adjective lists for classifying music, see Paul R. Farnsworth, *The Social Psychology of Music*, New York: The Dryden Press, 1958, pp. 95-99.

made to feel free to state their own personal feelings concerning
mood, even when they may differ from those expressed by the
majority of the group.

Imagery.   Imagery [5] is a flexible topic for a listening lesson
suitable for most all grade levels. The teacher may ask the
children the question, "What does the music remind you of?" or
"How does the music make you feel?" Such an approach provides an excellent stimulant to the creative mind. Imagination
is certainly one trait that needs to be nurtured in children in as
many ways as possible. Another approach is for the teacher to
encourage the students to create stories about what they feel the
music says. Here the listening lesson may be closely correlated
with the objectives of the language arts class, where one objective of the teacher is the development of skills in both oral and
written English. Utilizing music in connection with these studies
provides a strong motivating force or stimulant for such activities. Art teachers, as well as classroom teachers, also use music
for this purpose. For initial experiences in creative art work the
teacher should provide a brief over-view of the background of
the music (sometimes even a title is enough). In some instances,
he will refrain from mentioning the title or describing the music
in any way. Therefore, the children will not have any restrictions
or limitations placed upon the topic or scope of their drawings.
By this approach, certain students have been encouraged to
create some especially interesting abstract drawings.

Following are some suggested recordings of music which are
excellent for listening lessons pertaining to the development of
imagery.

> "Dance of the Comedians" (from *The Bartered Bride*)
>   by Bedrich Smetena
> "Dance Macabre" by Camille Saint-Saëns
> "Night on Bald Mountain" by Modest Mussorgsky
> "A Summer Day" by Serge Prokofiev (Young People's
>   Records). With this particular recording, for example,

5 Imagery may be defined as the mental likeness or picture of an
object, idea, or concept.

the teacher may say, "As you listen you will hear many different sounds and various moods. Close your eyes and put your imaginations to work. We will discuss your reactions to the music after we have heard it."

Aural recognition of orchestral instruments.   The aural recognition of various band and orchestral instruments is an important and integral part of the listening program. Development of the child's ability to recognize the timbre, or distinctive tonal characteristics, of various instruments can contribute substantially to his enjoyment of future listening experiences. It is suggested that children be introduced to this topic in either the second or third grade (depending upon their background and level of musical development). The recording, "The Child's Introduction to the Orchestra and all its Instruments" (Golden Record No. GLP:1), is suggested for these beginning experiences.[6] The first part of the section devoted to each instrument utilizes a story sung by a singer who describes the characteristics of the instrument and the position each holds in its respective family in the orchestra. The second part of each section features the instrument in a presentation of music from the standard solo or orchestral literature. After the children are reasonably acquainted with the instruments from listening to the record and through seeing pictures or demonstrations of actual instruments, they may be asked to identify particular instruments as the second part only of the record is played. Instruments should generally be introduced by families, *i.e.,* strings, woodwinds, and brass. The first attempt at identifying specific instruments should also be by families. Later, after the children have progressed in their ability to recognize these various instruments, the teacher may select at random various instruments in the series and ask the children to identify them.

For children in the intermediate grades the following recordings may also be used to further broaden their understanding of and ability to recognize the various instruments.

---

[6] Available through local dealers, or through Affiliated Publishers, 630 Fifth Avenue, New York, N.Y. 10020.

"Instruments of the Orchestra" (Columbia, Decca, RCA Victor)

"Meet the Instruments," filmstrips also available. (Bowmar Records)

"Young Person's Guide to the Orchestra" by Benjamin Britten (Capitol)

Records which present a story about musical instruments are excellent for motivational as well as for instructional purposes. While they may be considered as supplementary to the previously mentioned records, they are essential to a well-rounded listening program. Some of these titles are as follows:

"Tubby the Tuba" (Decca)

"Pee Wee the Piccolo" (RCA Camden)

"Rusty in Orchestraville" (Capitol)

"Said the Piano to the Harpsichord" (Young People's Records) [7]

"The Wonderful Violin" (Young People's Records)

Components of music.   Music contains four basic components —melody, rhythm, harmony, and tone color.

A *melody* is a succession of single related tones within a particular mode or key. A good melody has a beginning, a middle, and an end, yet its contour or shape may be perceived as a whole. Melody has a strange power which causes one to hum or sing whenever it comes to mind.

Rhythm is the organization of tones in regard to their length or duration. Rhythm is that aspect of the music that sometimes elicits a bodily response, such as tapping one's foot to the music of a marching band. Rhythm, however, may vary in nature from the obvious and regularly recurrent stresses of a march to the more subtle rhythm of a trill.

Harmony is the relationship of chords and their progression or movement from one to another. Harmony adds depth and perspective to the music, and enhances the melodic line. Children will have experienced the effect of harmony in the

----

[7] For additional titles in this series, see *Teachers' Annotated Catalog of the Children's Record Guild* and *Young People's Records,* p. 14.

piano accompaniment to their songs. In the intermediate grades they will have had the opportunity for vocal chording. (See Chapter 8, which will provide the basis for studying chord relationships.)

Tone Color, or timbre, is the unique tonal characteristic of a particular instrument or voice which enables the listener to distinguish it from others. The combination of all the varied tonal colors may be compared to the artist's palette. The composer may, through combining, blending, and contrasting these various timbres, create the musical effects he wishes.

Each of the above terms should be clarified for intermediate grade students in a reasonably straight-forward way, first by simple explanation, then by musical examples followed by ample discussion. Certainly, music speaks for itself and a good musical example is worth many words. Discussion following the listening session, however, will serve to clarify in the students' minds what they have heard and will provide the teacher with a way to determine the degree of their understanding. This approach may provide the basis for numerous subsequent listening lessons. For the initial listening experiences, however, it is essential to select music in which the predominate component is fairly obvious. Following are some suggested examples.

Rhythm:
  "Rackocsky March" by Hector Berlioz
  "Marche Militaire" by Franz Schubert
  "Rite of Spring" by Igor Stravinsky
Melody:
  "Ave Maria" by Franz Schubert
  "Symphony No. 6" (Pathetique), First Movement by Peter Ilich Tschaikovsky
Harmony:
  "Kom Süsser Tod" (Come Sweet Death) by J. S. Bach
  "Rejoice, Ye Christians Loudly" by J. S. Bach
  "Prelude" to *Tristan and Isolde* by Richard Wagner
Tone Color:
  "Scheherezade" by Nicolai Rimsky-Korsakov
  "La Mer" (The Sea) by Claude Debussy
  "Daphnis and Chloe" (Suite No. 2) by Maurice Ravel

Styles of articulation.   The three basic styles of articulation are *legato* (smooth and connected), *staccato* (short and detached), and *marcato* (marked or well-accented). Whereas a great proportion of music contains combinations of all three styles, there are many examples available in which one style of articulation is predominant throughout. For children to learn to identify these styles by listening can be a very desirable experience. Prior to listening, the teacher should write the words *legato, staccato,* and *marcato* on the chalkboard, explain their meaning, and provide some examples for purposes of clarification.[8] A suggested further procedure is for the class to sing a song, such as "America," which is in a *legato* style, then to sing it in a detached *staccato* style, and finally in a *marcato* style. Of course, the singing of "America" in either of the latter two styles will seem awkward and inappropriate. For this reason the procedure is one of the best ways for developing a reasonably quick understanding of differences between these three basic styles of articulation. It would also be helpful if music basically requiring either *staccato* or *marcato* styles of articulation could also be sung in all three ways. The change from the natural and correct style to a contrasting different style helps to reinforce the point the teacher is trying to make.

Form in music.   Form refers to the general shape or architecture of the music. It has sometimes been referred to as the skeleton of music, that which gives it its over-all shape. The possibilities for listening lessons based on this topic are unlimited, since all music has form which may be analyzed by some means or other. Following are some of the types of musical form, and examples of each, appropriate for study and analysis in the intermediate grades.

1. *Binary form* is a form consisting of two contrasting, but stylistically related sections, usually outlined as AB or AABB. The binary, or two-part form may consist of two relatively short parts, as found in many songs, or of two more extended sections,

---

8 The manner of articulation is usually dictated by the words or the text of the music. This is also an important point to stress.

as in certain piano and orchestra literature.[9] In introducing this form to children the simpler of the binary forms should be utilized. The following examples are suggested: [10]

> "America" by Henry Carey
> "Santa Lucia" (Italian folksong)
> "Lullaby" by Johannes Brahms (RCA Victor Listening Activities, Volume 1, E77)
> "Saraband," from *Suite for Strings* by Arcangelo Corelli (Adventures in Music, Grade 6, Volume 2, RCA Victor)
> "Non Presto" from the *Good-Humored Ladies* by Domenico Scarlatti. (Adventures in Music, Grade 4, Volume 2, RCA Victor).

2. *Ternary form* is in three parts, generally stated or outlined as ABA. The first section (A) is followed by a contrasting middle section (B), in turn followed by a restatement of the original section (A). Examples of this form may be found in music ranging from folk and popular songs to more extended works. In songs, the first part is generally repeated, followed by a contrasting section, and ending with a repetition of the first part. Examples of music to use with intermediate grade students are as follows:

> "The Ash Grove" (Welsh folksong)
> "Drink to Me only with Thine Eyes" (Old English Air)
> "Circus Music" from *The Red Pony* by Aaron Copland (Adventures in Music, Grade 3, Volume 1, RCA Victor).
> "Children's Symphony," First Movement, by Harl McDonald (Adventures in Music, Grade 3, Volume 2, RCA Victor).

[9] For examples of these more serious works, see Gordon Goewey and John Kucaba, *Understanding Musical Form*, Dubuque, Iowa: Wm. C. Brown Company, Publishers, 1962.

[10] Songs listed as examples of simple binary and ternary forms may be found in *Songs for Every Purpose and Occasion*, Minneapolis: Schmitt, Hall & McCreary, 1938.

"March" from *Ballet Suite* by Jean-Baptiste Lully (Adventures in Music, Grade 3, Volume 2, RCA Victor)

"Hoe-Down" from *Rodeo—Ballet Suite* by Aaron Copland (Adventures in Music, Grade 5, Volume 2, RCA Victor).

3. *Rondo* is a form in which the original theme "returns" following a number of "digressions" or statements of contrasting melodic material. Various rondo forms may be outlined as ABACA, ABACADA, or ABACABA. In presenting this particular form the teacher should first make sure that the students are familiar with the principal theme. This process is often facilitated if the theme is written on the chalkboard and sung by the class. Before playing a particular composition, however, the teacher should ask the class to keep track of the number of times the main theme returns following a digression. They may be asked to raise their hands upon the "return" or simply to "keep score" by themselves. The procedure used, of course, will depend upon the general ability of the class. Subsequent discussion may focus upon the nature of the digressions. Following are some examples of rondo form that may be used with intermediate grade students.

"Gavotte" (from the opera *Mignon*) by Thomas (ABACABACA Codetta) (RCA Victor Rhythm Band Album, E90)

"Minuet in G" by Ignace Paderewski (ABACABA Coda) (RCA Victor Rhythm Band Album, E90)

"Pirouette" by Herman Finck (ABACBA Codetta) (RCA Victor Rhythm Band Album, Volume E90)

"Waltz on the Ice" from *Winter Holiday* by Sergei Prokofiev (ABACA Coda) (Adventures in Music, Grade 3, Volume 2, RCA Victor)

"Grand Walk-Around" from *'Cakewalk' Ballet Suite* by Louis Moreau Gottschalk (ABABACA Coda) (Adventures in Music, Grade 5, Volume 1, RCA Victor)

"Rondo for Bassoon and Orchestra" by Weber (Young People's Records, No. 1009)

"Rondo, Piano Sonata in D Major" by Franz Joseph Haydn (ABACA)

4. *Theme and variations* is a form utilizing a statement of a theme followed by a number of variations of this theme that are still recognizable, but altered by changes in rhythm, harmony, or melodic line. The number of variations may range from two (as in the first example below) to thirty or more. Students should be reasonably acquainted with the principal theme before the music is played. Prior to listening, they should be asked to keep track of the number of variations and to be prepared to describe the manner in which the main theme was changed in each of the variations. The below are good examples for use with intermediate grade children.

> "Theme and Two Variations" by Enrique Granados in *Meet Modern Music,* Part Two. New York: Mercury Music Corporation. (Excellent for the initial demonstration of this form.)
> "Variations on the Theme, 'Pop Goes the Weasel' " by Lucien Cailliet. (Adventures in Music, Grade 4, Volume 1, RCA Victor.)
> "American Salute" by Morton Gould (Adventures in Music, Grade 5, Volume 1, RCA Victor).
> "The Girl I Left Behind Me" from *Irish Suite* by Leroy Anderson (Adventures in Music, Grade 5, Volume 2, RCA Victor.)
> "Symphony No. 94 in G" ("Surprise" Second Movement) by Franz Joseph Haydn.[11]

Other listening specifics.   The preceding topics for listening lessons comprise a basic list of experiences for all children which will assist them in achieving a better understanding of music. Beyond this point the teacher may ask the class to listen for a variety of other specifics. For example, they may be asked to

[11] A line score of this music (theme and four variations) may be found in Guy A. Bockmon and William J. Starr, *Scored for Listening: A Guide to Music,* New York: Harcourt, Brace, and World, Inc., 1959, pp. 167-169.

listen for distinctive rhythmic patterns in the music, differences between major and minor modes, contrasting pitch levels, the use of particular solo instruments, contrasting types of accompaniment, wide melodic leaps, dissonant effects, musical embroidery such as trills, grace notes, etc., the differences between minor scales, changing key centers, changes in texture, and many other topics.

For appropriate listening materials to achieve these objectives the Basic Record Library *Adventures in Music* (10 albums, RCA Victor), is particularly recommended. The *Teacher's Guide*,[12] prepared by Gladys and Eleanor Tipton, sets forth in considerable detail procedures for guiding the student's attention to the musical specifics mentioned above.

Encouraging "out-of-school" listening

Certainly one primary objective of the school listening program is to encourage boys and girls to listen to both recorded music and actual concerts during their out-of-school hours. The extent to which children listen outside of school might even be considered as one measure of the success of the school listening program. It is one thing to develop a well-rounded school listening program and another for boys and girls to demonstrate the desire to listen to music when they are not a captive audience. The mere existence of a listening program does not necessarily insure that boys and girls will take advantage of the many opportunities for outside listening while they are in school and in later life. Teachers, therefore, should take some definite steps toward the accomplishment of this goal. Following are some essential points for consideration.

Encourage children to bring their recordings to school. While not all students in a given class will possess their own

---

[12] Individual manuals of the *Teacher's Guide* may be purchased separately.

collection of recordings, some children do. These particular students should be asked to bring them to school and to share their listening experiences with classmates. Prior to playing the recording, the child should be asked to tell his classmates something about the music and the composer, and perhaps what it is about the record that particularly intrigues him. In addition to the sharing of a musical experience, considerable benefit accrues to the child from the experience of telling about his own record. Certain skills in speaking before others are furthered when the child has something of a personal nature to describe. In addition, his own status within the group is often raised, and the self-confidence which results can make a significant contribution to the child's personal and emotional growth.

At this point, the reader may think, "What should the teacher do about records which are not too appropriate from the musical standpoint or to the objectives of the music class?" This problem may be handled by the teacher in his initial statement: "Some of you boys and girls have recordings which I am sure you would like to share in our listening sessions with the class. Some of these recordings would be most helpful in the study of our present topic. If you have recordings which you particularly enjoy and would like to share with the class, why don't you make a list of the titles and composers and the performing group and bring it to me. Then I will be able to select the ones which will be most appropriate to our class work." The preceding statement lays the groundwork for group understanding of the fact that only certain types of music are germane to the objectives of the class and that the teacher must use his best judgment in the selection process. Handling the matter this way will generally minimize any problems of children bringing to class recordings of music inappropriate to its needs. Furthermore, students are generally cognizant of the teacher's responsibility in many areas. This approach need not conflict at all with the philosophy of allowing the children an opportunity to participate in determining the general areas and scope of study in a particular unit.

Call attention to radio and television programs.   The teacher should make a definite effort to call to the students' attention noteworthy musical programs on radio and television. Radio stations in certain localities present various musical programs of a worthwhile nature. While at the present time television does not carry an extensive number of "high level" programs on music, there are, nevertheless, a few notable programs of considerable merit. For example, the Leonard Bernstein programs are extremely worthwhile and are generally of great interest to school children. Periodically there are also other programs from which the children can derive considerable benefit. In terms of maintaining the interest of children, television has an advantage over radio in that it presents not only the aural element but the visual as well. It is hoped that the television industry will take stock of its present status and endeavor in the future to raise the level of existing programs and to schedule more musical programs of a worthwhile nature.

It is suggested that teachers maintain a bulletin board and post notices of various programs, as well as announcing them in class. It is felt that some programs should be "required" listening for all the students in the class. Children will be more likely to remember to listen if, prior to the program, the teacher discusses with them what they are to hear, and then following the program discusses in class what they actually heard, and, of course, what they liked about it. By making the programs a more integral part of the class work, the children will also gain much more from these listening experiences.

Encourage attendance at concerts.   In most communities, concerts of some type are usually available to the general public. These programs or concerts may range from those presented through the auspices of the Cooperative Concert Association to programs given by local groups—by schools, churches, and community musical organizations. Again, posting notices of these programs on the bulletin board, announcing them in class, and discussing them with the children following the concert are all suggested means of encouraging attendance.

Other aspects of the listening program

The total school listening program is much broader in scope than merely listening to teacher-selected recordings in the classroom. Following are some other broad areas which the teacher should consider.

Utilizing "live" music. Whenever possible, the teacher should endeavor to utilize "live" music in the classroom, or in the auditorium, for the benefit of the entire school. While recordings hold a considerable degree of interest for children, they cannot be expected to stimulate the same degree of interest as will live performers. Most all communities possess a number of potential program possibilities. Classroom teachers should discuss their needs with both their principal and music supervisor or consultant. Inquiries may be directed to the music teachers in a nearby junior or senior high school. The vocal and instrumental music teachers in these schools are generally desirous of providing opportunities for their musical organizations to perform. They are also cognizant of the importance of stimulating musical interest in their future students.

Perhaps the band, orchestra, or choir can be brought to the school for an assembly program. If these organizations cannot be conveniently scheduled, then consideration should be given to small vocal or instrumental ensembles or various soloists. Certainly all secondary school students will derive benefit by performing before other school audiences.

In addition to nearby secondary schools, the teachers should also consider that students in the music department of a local college or university may also be secured to present programs of a varied nature, preferably in the classroom. Also, various adult musical organizations often exist in the community which may be invited to present programs in the school.

Finally, the teacher should not overlook the possibilities which exist in his own school. In any one school, there are generally a number of exceptionally talented children who are able and willing to share their musical talents with fellow students. Certainly of all types of live performers, the latter is often the most interesting to school children. To be able to hear one's own peers perform musically is a treat which most children cannot forget.

Utilizing community resources.   In almost all communities there are a number of valuable resources which the classroom teacher should endeavor to take advantage of by means of the "field trip" or class visit. Such visits may provide valuable information and contribute to student motivation. They also provide a common basis or background for written and oral expression in the language arts. Field trips, of course, should always be arranged through the school office. The principal and the music supervisor can also often provide helpful suggestions in terms of where, when (the suggested hours), and how long to visit. Following are some of the places which teachers will wish to consider for possible field trips.

1. A trip to a nearby church to hear a lecture-demonstration by the church organist can prove of considerable interest and benefit to children. Most boys and girls do not have the opportunity to develop a genuine appreciation of the organ as a musical instrument. They are often totally unaware of the variety of tonal color combinations inherent in this instrument and often think of the organ as only a background to the church service. In other words, their understanding and appreciation of this instrument are somewhat limited. What better way is there to develop an appreciation of an instrument than in the company of one's peers? Boys and girls enjoy doing things together and often assume the likes and dislikes of their friends. If the background and maturity of the children are carefully considered in planning the presentation, such a visit may contribute substantially to the development of a lasting interest and appreciation of the organ as a musical instrument.

2. Motion picture theaters all have a considerable investment in audio equipment that is vastly superior to anything the schools could ever hope to possess because of the limitations of

cost. Listening to a stereophonic recording through the audio equipment in a neighborhood theater can provide an exciting listening adventure for students. Again, listening experiences in the company of one's peers often provides the framework for a desirable learning situation. Teachers will find that most theater managers are quite responsive to a request to visit. They are willing in most cases to accommodate teachers and students with such requests because of the desirable public relations values which accrue to them and to their theaters.

3. Museums sometimes have a collection of ancient instruments, which would be of considerable interest to children. Music teachers often utilize special units of study on the instruments of the orchestra. Following this unit of study a worthwhile topic would be the study of instruments which preceded orchestral instruments as we know them today. Classroom teachers who teach specific units on the development of civilization will in particular find that such a field trip provides considerable motivation for the study of various topics. In addition, a great deal of interest will be developed in regard to instruments in general.

4. Taking a trip to a local radio or television station to observe first-hand the vast library of recordings, the recording and playback equipment, turntables, and so forth, can be most enlightening to children. Whereas one might question the basic musical values from such a visit, it should be mentioned that some persons' appreciation of music has originally stemmed, not from the aesthetic qualities of music, but from the technical aspects of recording and broadcasting. From an initial appreciation of the characteristics of good technical equipment some persons are often led into an appreciation of the aesthetic qualities of music. In the final analysis it is important not where one begins, but where one ends.

5. Attending a music concert in the community as a class project may be a stimulating experience for boys and girls because of the motivational values of experiencing a concert in the company of their friends. Of course, the musical values of such programs are of prime consideration and should not be overlooked.

Motion picture films.   Another very important aspect of the school listening program is the utilization of selected motion picture films pertaining to music. A wide variety of topics are available for showing, including films on various performing groups, composers, music theory, vocal techniques, and even films on music reading and part singing. Films have the added impact of the visual in addition to the aural aspect of music. They provide considerable interest and motivation among students of all age groups. Titles may often be located which pertain to the topic or unit of study in which the class is currently engaged. For sources which list a variety of films appropriate for classroom use, the following publications are suggested:

> *Film Guide for Music Educators.* Donald A. Shetler, Washington, D. C.: Music Educators National Conference, 1961.
> *Educational Film Guide.* New York: The H. W. Wilson Company.
> *Conducting Choral Music,* Second Edition. Robert L. Garretson. Boston: Allyn and Bacon, Inc., 1965, pp. 291-300.

Informal listening.   Periodically it is desirable to organize, in cooperation with the students, an informal listening session principally just to "have fun." Perhaps once a month or so, the students in the class should perform for each other. Some may sing solos, or organize duets or trios. Others might play instrumental selections of their own choice. The purpose of such a listening session is to allow the students the opportunity to organize for themselves a classroom concert which features the talents of the members of the class, thus removing the formality of class study and allowing the class to concentrate upon sheer listening enjoyment.

A listening corner.   The establishment of a "listening corner" is a highly recommended practice for all schools. The teacher should set aside one part of the classroom and install a record player with multiple headsets through which a number of children can listen simultaneously to recordings without disturbing the rest of the class. Children may often listen before or after school without disturbing the on-going activity which is likely to be occurring in most classrooms. A prevalent practice in most modern schools is the use of committee work, assigned on the basis of mutual interests. These particular committees, after a given period of time, report their findings to the class as a whole. Through this procedure the work of a given class is enriched to a considerable extent. With the flexibility of this arrangement, certain committees may wish to listen to a variety of music and select appropriate recordings which they include in their reports.

Purchasing equipment

The type of equipment existent in any one classroom is important to the outcomes of the school listening program. The teacher should have an ample supply of desirable and appropriate recordings, as well as a suitable record player. The following is an outline of the considerations which should be taken into account in acquiring a selection of recordings.

Criteria for selecting recordings
1. Purpose
   a. Listening
   b. Rhythmic activities
   c. Introduction and study of songs
2. Suitability
   a. Children's previous musical experience
   b. Adaptability to current unit of study and group interest
   c. Motivation for future learning experiences
3. Artistic value
   a. Inherent musical value
   b. Authenticity of rendition, correctness of style
4. Practicality
   a. Fidelity
   b. Durability
   c. Flexibility of uses

It is extremely difficult to develop any degree of appreciation of music through listening to recordings on a small, inexpensive record player which does not adequately reproduce the original sound to at least a reasonable degree. It is suggested that all classroom teachers who are responsible for including music in their teaching make an appropriate request for a suitable record player for their classrooms. It is desirable to have in each room a record player which retails for approximately one hundred and seventy-five to two hundred dollars. With a sizeable school discount, the cost of the equipment comes within a range which most schools should be able to afford. If the total cost is deemed unfeasible from the financial standpoint, then it would be far better to purchase one record player of a reasonably good quality than several less expensive ones. If casters are placed on the bottom of the cabinet, such a machine can be easily moved from room to room. To avoid conflicts in the use of this equipment, the teachers involved should meet together at the beginning of the year (or each semester) and outline a schedule which will meet the needs and demands of all those involved.

Topics for discussion

1. Discuss the twin statements, "learn to listen" and "listen to learn" as summarizations of the basic objectives of the listening program in the kindergarten-primary and the intermediate grades. To what extent do these statements correctly express one's objectives? In what ways are the statements inaccurate and misleading?

2. Discuss the three basic steps involved in guided listening.

3. Discuss the importance of the teacher as a factor in the listening process.

4. Discuss some general procedures for creating interest in music and for motivating children to listen carefully.

5.   In what ways can the teacher encourage out-of-school listening?

6.   In what ways can the teacher enlist the cooperation of parents in providing appropriate experiences in listening at home?

Suggestions for further study

ELLIOTT, Raymond. *Teaching Music: Methods and Materials for the Elementary Schools.* Columbus, Ohio: Merrill, 1960, Ch. 4.

HARTSHORN, William C. "The Role of Listening," Chapter 11 in *Basic Concepts in Music Education.* The fifty-seventh Yearbook of the National Society for the Study of Education. Chicago: Univ. of Chicago Press, 1958.

MYERS, Louise Kifer. *Teaching Children Music in the Elementary School,* 3rd ed. Englewood Cliffs, N.J.: Prentice-Hall, 1961, Ch. 6.

SWANSON, Bessie R. *Music in the Education of Children.* 2nd ed. Belmont, Calif.: Wadsworth, 1964, Ch. 8.

Films

Design To Music (International Film Bureau, 332 S. Michigan Ave., Chicago, Ill. 60604), 1949, color, 6 min. Elem./Col.

Sounds of Music, The (Coronet Instructional Films, 65 E. South Water St., Chicago, Ill.), 1948, b&w or color, 10 min. Discusses the physics of sound. Elem.

5 Experiences with instruments

~~~~~~~~~~~~~~~~~~~~~~~~~~~~~~~~~~

The playing of instruments is an integral part of the modern school music program. Experience with musical sound in various media can contribute substantially to children's musical development. All children enjoy experimenting with musical sound; and those who have not found their voices, and have developed a certain timidity as a result, may be drawn to music through the manipulative aspects of playing instruments. Skills in music reading may be facilitated through the study of and experience with instruments. Understanding of the durational aspects of music may be enhanced through experience with rhythm instruments, and the intervalic experience of solfeggio may be reinforced through playing certain melody and chord or harmony instruments. Keyboard instruments, such as the piano, especially help children to see, as well as hear, the relationship between the various scale steps. Each instrument, however, has its unique values and makes its contribution to the child's musical development.

Experimenting with sounds of various media

Children especially enjoy experimenting with the sounds which may be produced by various common materials—

glasses, bottles, cardboard boxes, wooden boxes, metal pipes and nails, twine or cord, heavy rubber bands, flower pots, pans and other kitchen utensils, and many other materials. In addition to exploring the unique sounds of these materials, children will also be intrigued by the differences in the sound of objects of the same material but of varying sizes. Simple explanations of these differences in quality and pitch should be provided the children when the teacher feels they are *receptive* to and may comprehend the information. Class discussions on this topic are particularly appropriate for first grade children and provide an excellent preparatory experience to the later playing of other simple instruments.

Water glasses, for example, may be utilized for the playing of simple melodies. They may be tuned to different pitches by varying the amount of water placed in them. The pitch of each glass may be sounded by striking it lightly on the side with a spoon or a nail. For the initial experiences for first grade children, three glasses will suffice for the playing of simple tunes, involving, of course, only three pitches. Glasses should be carefully selected and those utilized should produce a reasonably clear tone. (A thin glass is generally preferable to a thicker one.) Glasses without water will produce varying pitches when struck with an object. Therefore, first test the glasses and use the one that gives the highest pitch for the top note. This is especially important if an entire scale of eight tones is to be prepared. When water is added to the glass the pitch will descend—that is, the more water the lower the pitch. For the tuning process it is desirable to have available a pitcher of water, so that small amounts may be added to the glass at a time. First, add sufficient water to the first glass to give it the desired pitch. This will be considered *do,* or the first scale tone. Next add a sufficient amount of water to the second glass until it sounds a whole step up, or *re.* Likewise, tune the third glass to *mi,* a whole step up from the second glass. It is a good idea to place a small piece of tape on each glass to indicate the desired water level so that that the glasses can be kept "in tune" during continual use and prepared more easily for subsequent use. The teacher may, at first, briefly demonstrate how the glasses are tuned. The children should note that when water is added the pitch lowers, and when water is removed from the glasses the pitch rises. (The pitch becomes higher as the vibrating body becomes smaller, lower as the body grows larger.) A simple explanation may accompany the teacher's demonstration if he feels that the children will be able to comprehend the information. In general, however, it is better to tune the glasses prior to the lesson. The children are liable to become restless with the delay of a long tuning demonstration.

For initial experiences with the water glasses it is best to select simple tunes involving only three pitches. Suggested examples are "Hot Cross Buns" and "Mary Had a Little Lamb" (alter the fifth scale step to a third).[1] Both these tunes are familiar to most first graders, having been learned in kindergarten or during their pre-school years. After the teacher has played the tune at least once, it should be repeated with the entire class singing. Then, a few children may be asked to play the glasses. Some first graders may accomplish this task perfectly—others will have some difficulty, but only by trying will they learn.

For subsequent experiences, the teacher and pupils may wish to build a diatonic scale of eight tones. For this it is preferable to use bottles rather than glasses. Quart size soda bottles are generally quite adequate for this purpose. They may be tuned in the same procedure as previously suggested, *i.e.,* by selecting the desired top or high pitch in the scale and tuning it with the necessary amount of water, then adding proportional amounts of water for the lower pitches. After the bottles have been tuned, they should be stopped with a cork to prevent the water from spilling and from evaporating. It is still desirable, however, to indicate the desired water level of each bottle with a piece of adhesive tape. Although evaporation will be slight, it will occur and for subsequent use they may be checked much more readily. For ease in playing, each bottle may be suspended with cord or wire from a wooden or metal (pipe) stand constructed for this purpose. This fixture can be easily made in the school shop. A height of approximately five feet is suggested

---

[1] Other suggested songs are "Night Song" (German folk tune), *Birchard Music Series, Book Two,* p. 110; and "Pierrot's Door" (first part).

for the stand. The lengths of cord for each bottle may then be adjusted so that each bottle may be easily struck by the majority of children in the class. (It is suggested that each bottle be about chest high.) A simple alternative, until such a stand can be constructed, is to suspend the bottles from a $\frac{3}{4}'' \times 1\frac{1}{2}''$ board about four feet in length. The board may be suspended between two tables (the higher the better). With this arrangement the children will, in most cases, have to play the bottles while seated.

Exploring the sounds made by striking together various types and sizes of wood is a worthwhile project of considerable interest and value to children. There are differences in *pitch* between small and large sticks as they are struck together, and differences in *quality* between small and large blocks of wood as they are clapped together, and between varieties of soft and hard wood of similar sized objects—all of these are sounds which should be explored.

Varying sizes of wooden and cardboard boxes may be struck, in the manner of a drum, with a mallet or beater or with the hand. The differences in pitch and in quality should be observed. Children should also experiment by striking the boxes in various places—in the center and near the edges. Various rhythmic patterns may be played on the sticks, boxes, and blocks. Some of these items may even be later incorporated as a part of the instruments of the rhythm band.

The sounds made by striking various types and sizes of metal together should also be explored. Large nails, railroad spikes, and pieces of metal pipe may be struck together and the differences in quality of sound noted. Metal triangles may be made from heavy wire (or coathangers), metal tubing, small piping, and solid iron bars (for reinforcing concrete). These materials may be placed in a vise and without too much difficulty shaped into a triangle. They should be suspended with a cord or string so that the sound is not dampened. A large nail makes an excellent beater. All of these materials may also be later incorporated as instruments of the rhythm ensemble.

Young children will also enjoy investigating the sounds that can be made by plucking a taut cord or a heavy rubber band. The cord or rubber band may be lengthened or shortened and the subsequent difference in pitch noted. Such a demonstration may provide a reasonably simple and straight-forward explanation as to how the various string instruments work, *i.e.*, pitch depends upon the tension and length of the vibrating body.

Experience with rhythm instruments

Experience with rhythm or percussion instruments has many values for children: it may reinforce concepts of pitch and duration; it increases the child's awareness of differences in timbre; it may facilitate more careful listening habits; it improves individual response to pulse and accent; and it broadens the child's experiences with rhythm and furthers his perceptiveness of the differences in rhythmic patterns.

A former practice, now outmoded, was for the teacher to carefully rehearse and drill the rhythm ensemble to "perfection." The result of such a teacher dominated activity was a "rhythm

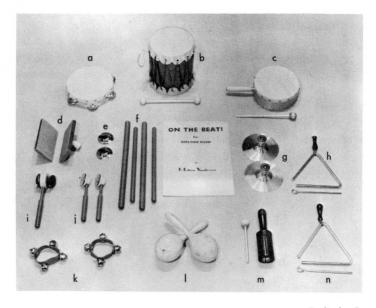

Peripole, Inc.

A basic set of Rhythm instruments: (a) tambourine, (b) tom tom drum, (c) snare drum, (d) sand blocks, (e) finger cymbals, (f) rhythm sticks, (g) cymbals, (h) triangles, (i) castanets with handle, (j) jingle clogs, (k) wrist bells, (l) gourd maracas, (m) tone block and mallet.

band" of musical robots, who were afforded little opportunity for genuine musical growth. A varied and creative approach to the use of rhythm instruments is necessary today if they are to fulfill an educational purpose.

Basic rhythm instruments

Rhythm band activities are particularly appropriate for children in the kindergarten-primary grades but, under certain circumstances, their use may be continued with older children. Young children are intrigued by instruments of all types, and over a period of time should be provided experience with all rhythm instruments. The basic rhythm band instruments are as follows:

tom tom drum	jingle clogs
snare drum	finger cymbals
tambourine	sand blocks
gong	rhythm sticks
cymbals	castanets (on a handle)
triangle	wood (or tone) block
wrist bells	maracas
jingle bells (on a stick)	

It is highly important that the rhythm instruments used produce a reasonably good tone quality, otherwise their value is minimized. Basic sets of the instruments may be purchased from various companies specializing in such equipment. While some teachers prefer that students make their own instruments because it is a valuable creative effort, it is nevertheless desirable for the school to purchase a basic set to serve as a model for the "homemade" variety of instruments and to ensure that certain instruments in the total group possess an adequate tone quality.

Introducing rhythm instruments.   Rhythm instruments may best be introduced over an extended period of time, thus allowing ample opportunity for the exploration and discovery of each instrument's unique tonal characteristics. In this process, children may be led to an understanding that various instruments have differing pitches and durations of sound. They will discover, for example, that the tom tom drum has a low pitch in contrast to the triangle, which has a higher pitch. They will also discover

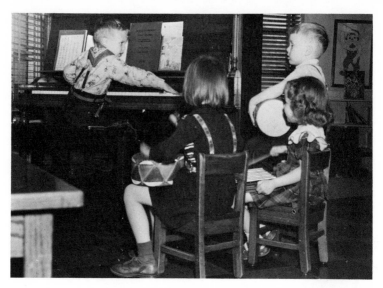

The University School, Indiana University, and
The Daily Herald-Telephone, Bloomington, Ind.

Young children enjoy the freedom of experimenting with different instruments.

that the drum and triangle resounds longer than does either the rhythm sticks or the jingle clogs. These understandings serve to reinforce the concepts of pitch and duration presented to young children through other means. (See pp. 34-37; 167-170.)

In the process of introducing the various instruments, each may be appropriately used as an accompaniment to songs with which the class is familiar. The teacher should never dictate the use of particular instruments, but set up learning situations where the children are allowed the opportunity to make discriminating choices. The children may choose, for example, to use the woodblock for "galloping" songs; the triangle and bells for songs depicting lightness of character, such as those about "rain" or "fairies"; and wrist bells and jingle bells to depict Christmas "sleigh bells." Instruments may also be used to accompany bodily movement. The children may wish to use the sand blocks to simulate "trains," or "shuffling feet"; the snare drum for "marching soldiers," and the tom tom drum for Indian dances.

Various combinations of instruments may also be used to accompany selected songs. For the specific purpose of reinforcing concepts of duration, one group of instruments may be played on the notes that move with the beat ($\quarternote$), another on the notes that move faster than the beat ($\eighthnotes$), and still another on the notes that move slower than the beat ($\halfnote$). (See p. 182 for an illustration of this idea.)

After children have had ample experience with the preceding exploratory activities, rhythm instruments may be combined in still larger groups, initially for the purpose of developing sensitivity to appropriate dynamics, accent and meter. It is not always necessary, nor desirable, for the entire class to play; rather, the use of smaller groups playing alternately has merit in that the "listening" group may serve as "critics." While the players may benefit from appropriate and helpful comments from their peers, the "critics" have the opportunity to develop, through careful listening, an increased sensitivity to the requirements of ensemble playing.

It is generally a desirable practice to ask the children to refrain from playing their instruments until the entire group is ready and they are told to begin. Holding the instruments in one's hand is too much a temptation, even for adults; to avoid unnecessary noise and confusion, the children should be asked to place the instruments under their seats and leave them there until the group is ready to play. Of course, there is something to be said for the value of student experimentation prior to group playing; however, as a means of preserving the teacher's "sanity" and in consideration of teachers and pupils in adjoining rooms, it is suggested that the above practice be followed.

For the initial ensemble experience the teacher should carefully select a recording or a piano selection which has a strong rhythmic pulsation. Before the children ever play their instruments they should listen carefully to the music as it is played completely through. The focus of the learning situation, at this point, is away from the instruments and toward the music. This is the proper beginning because, as the instruments are subsequently played, the children's response should emanate from or be influenced by the tempo, meter, pulsation, rhythmic patterns, dynamics, and phrasing of the music which they have just heard.

In the normal course of events, the children will quite naturally desire to focus their attention upon the instruments. However, if the proper outcomes of the activity are to be achieved, the teacher will necessarily have to redirect the children's attention to the music—sometimes quite frequently.

Before playing the recording again, the teacher should ask the class to respond with their instruments in some musically appropriate manner. Most students will probably play "on the beat." However, some may endeavor to play the rhythmic patterns in the music. The past experience of numerous teachers enables one to predict, with a reasonable degree of certainty, what the greatest problem will be during this initial playing. The children will undoubtedly be playing too loudly and will be too engrossed in the unique sounds of their instruments to listen to the music. Their attention should, therefore, be redirected toward it. The teacher might procede by questioning the class as to whether or not they could all hear the music. Some at least will reply in the negative. He may then pose the question, "Do you think the music should be played louder, or should you play your instruments more softly?" Most of the group will usually agree that they should perhaps play softer and listen more carefully. Some teachers might feel that, to save time, they should simply tell the class what to do. But experience has shown that the brief amount of time allotted to a discussion of the problem has resulted in an increased awareness of the problem on the part of the children. This awareness occurs to a much lesser extent when the teacher merely tells them what to do.

After the class has had the opportunity to concentrate upon the dynamics of their instruments and to focus their attention more directly upon the music, the teacher should ask them if some beats of the music sound louder than others. The class may be informed that this is what we call *accent*,[2] and that music is

2 The term *accent,* as it is referred to here, is regular accent, occurring as a stress at the beginning of each measure of the music. It should be understood, however, that accent may also be irregular; that is, it may occur at any point within the measure. For all practical purposes, however, this need not be discussed or raised with the children at this point unless some child (which is not likely) should ask about it.

grouped into, or swings in, "twos," "threes," or "fours." Another word for this is *meter*. Although the class may be vaguely aware of meter and some may be responding accordingly, they should have their attention directed toward it. The teacher may at this point play short portions of several selections and ask the class how the accents are grouped, that is, "how the music swings." After this has been determined, the class should be asked to take particular care to stress the appropriate places in the music when playing their instruments.

During subsequent rhythm activities, it will undoubtedly be noted that some children will be playing the rhythmic pattern of the music rather than responding simply to the basic pulse of the music. A discussion of this seemingly natural desire on the part of some students may be a beneficial learning experience for all. The teacher may remark: "I notice that all of the class is not playing the same way. What are some of you doing differently? Do you know why you want to do this?" Answers to these questions may be: "That is the way the music goes," or "It sounds better to play it that way." A discussion of this topic may lead the class to the realization that their rhythm ensemble might sound better if part of the group played the basic pattern (or pulsation) and the remainder played the rhythmic pattern of the music. A further level of differentiation may occur if the class is led into a discussion as to what instruments should play each of the different parts.

Developing further discrimination through orchestrations. A further ability to discriminate among the unique qualities of each instrument and the ability to relate or associate each with the mood, tempo, and other aspects of the music may be encouraged by having the students develop an "orchestration," or a plan for best distributing and utilizing the rhythm instruments on a particular musical selection.

One approach is for the group to play their instruments on various beats within the measure. For example, in music in quadruple meter, the class may first be asked to play on every beat (1, 2, 3, 4), then, on the first and third beats of the measure (1, —, 3, —), and then only on the first beat of the measure

(1, —, —, —,). As a means of maintaining strict time and responding precisely to the beat, the students should make a slight bodily or arm motion on the "silent beats," taking care not to sound the instrument which they are playing.

Next the class may be divided arbitrarily into three groups (perhaps the left, center, and right sides of the room) and each assigned to play a particular rhythmic pattern. One group may be assigned to play on every beat (1, 2, 3, 4), another on the first and third beats of the measure only (1, —, 3, —), and the remaining group on the first beat of each measure only (1, —, —, —,). Each group in the class should have the opportunity to play all of the patterns before the next step is taken.

Finally, rather than arbitrarily grouping the instruments according to portions of the room, the teacher should let the class determine through discussion what instruments sound best on the various beats. The instruments generally should be grouped together in families—that is, those instruments that have similar qualities or characteristics should be placed together. Any such classification should not be standard, and may vary from class to class. The important thing is, however, that the students, through adequate discussion and thought, give the matter proper consideration. Following is one possible grouping of instruments.

The orchestration which the students decide upon should be placed on the chalkboard so that the entire class may see it. It is often helpful if the notation is placed upon the board prior to the time the choices are made. This provides the class with an overall view of the three different patterns and may help them to decide which instruments should play each part. After all decisions have been made, the class may be re-seated according to the orchestration plan and should then have an opportunity to play what they have "orchestrated." Copies of these simple orchestrations may be duplicated, distributed to the class, and used at a later date for further rote-note reading experiences. It is also suggested that the teacher provide a similar experience using music in triple and duple meter. The following are patterns which the group or the teacher might notate on the chalkboard:

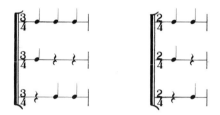

Another approach, requiring a slightly higher degree of differentiation, is for the class to "orchestrate" a familiar song. The class should begin by determining which group of instruments (perhaps as previously classified) would sound best on each of the phrases of the song. Various alternatives lie within each phrase: some instruments may play the melodic rhythm, some may play the basic pulsation of the music, while others may play on various designated beats of the measure. To be of optimum value to the students, their suggestions and decisions should be orchestrated on the chalkboard so that all may analyze it and make any changes they feel are necessary. After this has been done, the entire group should play the music through at least once, paying particular attention to the notation.

Some basic song texts include suggested orchestrations for rhythm instruments to accompany certain songs, such as the familiar "Old MacDonald," shown below. These will be found helpful in that they illustrate various alternative possibilities for the subsequent orchestration of other songs by the class.

Old MacDonald [3]
(Percussion Score)

In orchestrating songs, the students should be asked to follow the cue of the words, for through careful study of the text many subtle meanings and ideas appropriate for orchestration may be obtained. As a means of developing a wider range of tonal characteristics, the students may wish to abandon their former way of instrument grouping and seek another which will be more adaptable to the nuances of the text of the music. Classifying the instruments according to their characteristic sounds is one way in which the instruments may be grouped. Take, for example, the following list.

Characteristic sounds	*Instruments*
"clicking"	rhythm sticks
"tingling"	triangle, wristbells, jingle bells
"swishing"	sandblocks
"rattling"	jingle clogs, tambourine
"thumping"	drums, wood block
"crashing"	cymbals, gong

[3] From *This Is Music,* Book III, by William R. Sur, William R. Fischer, Mary R. Tolbert, and Adeline McCall. Copyright © 1961 by Allyn and Bacon, Inc. Used by permission.

While songs offer varied opportunities for orchestration, recorded instrumental music offers even wider possibilities. The RCA Victor Album, *Music for Rhythm Bands,* was prepared specifically for use with rhythm ensembles. In the front pages of the record album, suggested orchestrations are given for all the musical selections. While this information is exceedingly helpful, in that it provides a "model," students will benefit most from developing their own orchestrations. The selections, especially those in Rondo form, provide opportunity for considerable variety and creativeness in orchestrating.

Latin-American instruments

Various combinations of Latin-American instruments may be used as an accompaniment for particular songs and may also provide an effective rhythmic background for interpretive bodily movement. The varied uses of these instruments make them particularly appropriate to the level of maturity and the needs of intermediate grade students. Utilizing such instruments increases interest, enriches the total learning experience, and offers an opportunity to study various new rhythmic patterns. A basic list of recommended instruments is as follows:

claves	cowbells
maracas	bongo drums
guiro	conga drum
tubos (or shaker)	

Maracas are made either from carved wood or from gourds. They are approximately four inches in diameter and are equipped with handles. Each of the pair is filled with either pebbles, lead shot, or dried seeds. The maracas are shaken—one in each hand—in a short, precise, up-and-down movement. Perhaps a slightly simpler procedure for young children is to play only one maraca by rapping it against the palm of the hand.

The *tubos* (or shakers) is a long cylinder made from either metal or wood and filled with pebbles or dried seeds. It is played by holding each end and shaking either up and down or back and forth. The tonal effect is similar to that of the maracas.

Rhythm Band, Inc.

A Basic Set of Latin American Instruments: (a) **cowbell,** (b) **tambourine,** (c) **conga drum,** (d) **bongo drums,** (e) **guiro,** (f) **maracas,** (g) **claves,** (h) **tubos or shaker.**

The *claves* are two hardwood sticks approximately six inches in length and an inch in diameter. When struck together they produce a sharp yet resonant quality. One of the claves is held lightly in the left hand between the palm and the cupped fingers, while the other is held in the right hand between the thumb and the forefinger. In playing the claves, the one held in the right hand is used to strike the one in the left, which is held in a stationary position.

The *cowbell* is struck with a mallet and produces a dull, metallic tone. Cowbells are available in a variety of sizes ranging from four to seven inches. In the event a more muffled tone is desired, a small piece of adhesive tape may be placed inside the instrument.

The *guiro,* although generally made from carved wood, may also be made from a long-shaped gourd. Two small openings for securely holding the guiro are located on the bottom side-- one for the thumb and one for the index finger. The top side has a number of grooved notches. In playing, these notches are "scratched" with a stick in a rhythmical manner.

The *bongo drums* are relatively small and are joined to-gether with a wooden brace. One of the drums possesses a slightly higher pitch than the other. The drums should be placed be-tween the knees and played by striking one or two fingers against the drum heads.

The *conga drum* is a larger barrel-type drum and possesses a much deeper resonant tone than either of the bongo drums. It may be held between the knees while seated or suspended by a sling from the shoulder while standing.

Perhaps the best way to introduce the students to all these instruments is to utilize one or two as an accompaniment to a Latin-American folksong. The teacher should first demonstrate each instrument, emphasizing the manner in which it is held, describing the type of tone quality desired and the rhythmic patterns most appropriate to the particular instrument. These rhythmic patterns should be written on the chalkboard, analyzed and discussed, and then played. It is essential that the entire class participate actively in the study of these rhythmic pat-terns—they should *rap, tap,* or *clap* the patterns together. Cer-tain students may then be designated to play the rhythms as an accompaniment to a particular song. The teacher might ask the class to carefully examine the song and determine which of the patterns on the chalkboard seems to fit best. It is important that the teacher select rhythmic patterns for the initial demon-stration that *will* be adaptable to the chosen songs. In some in-stances, suggested rhythmic patterns for these instruments are included with the songs.[4] In such cases, the teacher might play the song on the piano and ask the class to make a choice of rhythmic patterns before they open their books. Of course, this procedure may be followed only if the class knows the song

[4] See, for example, *Music for Young Americans,* Books 5 and 6, New York: American Book Company, 1960; and *This Is Music,* Books 5 and 6, Boston: Allyn and Bacon, Inc., 1962.

quite well. In other instances, a quite different procedure may be utilized. The class should be asked to carefully examine the rhythmic patterns of a song and see if particular patterns inherent in it might be effectively used as an instrumental accompaniment.

After the class has had considerable experience in using the various Latin-American instruments, the entire group of instruments may be utilized as an accompaniment for certain selected songs. In addition, the instruments may form a percussion ensemble, which may be used as a rhythmic background for interpretive bodily movement. The following partial rhythm score may be duplicated or placed on the chalkboard for the entire group to study.

An alternative rhythmic pattern for the bongo drums is:

Experience with melody instruments

A variety of simple melody instruments is available which can contribute substantially to children's musical development. These may be classified into two basic groups—the bell or xylophone type, or those that are struck; and the simple wind instruments, those that are blown.

Simple wind instruments

The best known and least expensive of the simple wind instruments are the Flutophone, the Songflute, and the Tonette. When first introduced their value was thought of primarily as a preparation for the playing of regular band and orchestral instruments. Today these instruments are considered to have a broader and more basic educational value. The playing of such instruments necessitates that each child give thoughtful consideration to the proper manipulation necessary for effective playing. Experience with such instruments also assists in the improvement of the music reading process by reinforcing the response established through the use of syllables and/or numbers. The recorder may also be considered as a simple wind instrument.[5] Although slightly more expensive in initial cost and somewhat more difficult to play, it does have the advantage of a more extensive range (two octaves versus a ninth). Some teachers prefer to use the recorder exclusively, while others prefer to use the simpler instruments. Still other teachers like to use both, with the recorder being introduced after the children have had a year or so experience with one of the simpler instruments.[6] Since it is desirable that students own their own instruments, the teacher in making such a choice should consider the children's socio-economic background, as well as their previous musical experience and basic musical aptitude.

Introducing the instrument. In introducing a simple wind instrument the teacher should first demonstrate it by playing a

[5] The following Soprano Recorders are moderately priced and have proven practical for school use: Dolmetsch (plastic), Corelli (wooden), Ideal (wooden), Hohner Educator (wooden), and Aulos Standard—Toyama (plastic).

[6] A recommended plan is to use either the Flutophone, Songflute, or Tonette in the 4th grade and follow-up with the Recorder in the 5th and 6th grades.

Cincinnati Public Schools

Playing the Recorder, or other simple wind instruments, reinforces the intervalic relationships established through syllables and/or numbers.

simple tune, and then discuss with the class the principle of operation. That is, the sound is caused by a vibrating column of air and the longer the column the lower the pitch. The teacher should demonstrate to the class that as the holes are covered by the fingers from top to bottom the resonating column of air becomes longer and the pitch lower.

The correct manner of holding and blowing the instrument should also be stressed. The instrument is supported by placing the thumb of the right hand under the thumb rest, and should be held steady by the first finger of each hand. The left thumb should cover the hole on the back side of the instrument. The remaining three fingers of the left hand are used to cover the top three holes on the front of the instrument and the four fingers of the right hand to cover the bottom four openings. If this point is not stressed some students will invariably try to place the right hand above the left. This leads to a variety of problems and, therefore, the hand position of each child should be checked by the teacher at the outset. The mouthpiece should rest on the lower lip with the upper lip placed on the top of the mouthpiece. The teeth should not touch the mouthpiece. Only about half of the mouthpiece should be between the lips. As some students are inclined to insert too much and some too little of the mouthpiece, each individual student should be checked for the proper position.

In blowing the instrument only a minimum amount of air is needed. When children blow too hard (over-blow), false notes and noises are obtained which are generally a disrupting influence to the teaching procedure. To avoid this the teacher should stress from the outset the importance of blowing easily. In blowing, each note should be started as if saying the word "too." That is, the tip of the tongue touches the end of the mouthpiece lightly and then is drawn sharply back.

It is important that children have some facility with an instrument before they endeavor to begin the reading process; therefore, a semi-rote procedure is suggested in the beginning. Introduce "B" (third line, treble clef), as played with the thumb and first finger of the left hand and have the class play in the manner suggested above. Next, introduce "A" (thumb and two fingers in left hand) and then "G" (thumb and all three fingers in left hand). It is essential, at this point, for the teacher to stress the importance of carefully covering the holes necessary for playing each note. A procedure helpful in developing awareness of the function of the fingertips is to ask the class to press their fingers securely for several seconds on the finger holes, and then to look at the imprints on their finger tips. The teacher may play one of several simple tunes, such as "Hot Cross Buns" or "At Pierrot's Door," that necessitates only the use of these three tones. Following this experience, the teacher may introduce by rote the other remaining tones in the upper and lower register (C, D, and F, E, D, and C), and, at the close of this initial lesson, encourage the students to practice at home the tunes which they learned in class and to familiarize themselves with the other tones on the instrument.

Introducing notation.   At the beginning of the subsequent lesson, the teacher may place on the chalkboard the notation of the simple tunes which the class learned to play previously. The class may then be asked if they can identify the music. In the event they are unable to do so, the teacher should play the tune for them, after which he should explain that this is simply the notation for the music they have already learned to play. The letter names and the position of the notes on the staff should then be reviewed for the children's benefit, *e.g.,* "This note is B, and is played with the thumb and the first finger, this note is A, and so on." Following this review the students should play the tunes as the teacher points to each note. After these initial experiences, the students may be provided with the instruction books that include a progressive sequence of tonal and rhythmic problems.

Teaching procedures.   The teacher will want to use a variety of procedures in the teaching of simple wind instruments. In encountering a new musical selection the students should examine it carefully, looking for familiar and unfamiliar elements in the music. The teacher, after playing the music for the class, will explain the fingerings for new notes and clarify unfamiliar rhythmic patterns. After this, the class should attempt to play the music. When difficulties arise a combination of the following procedures may be used.

> 1. The students may be asked to sing the letter names of the music, while the teacher plays on his instrument. This serves to orient the group to the over-all configuration of the music, as well as providing practice in the identification of letter names.

2. The class may count the pulsation of the music (1, 2, 3, 4, etc.) as the teacher plays. This procedure helps those students who forget to count to themselves while playing.
3. The class and the teacher may clap the rhythm of the notation together.[7] (In general, rhythmic difficulties are a greater stumbling block than are fingering patterns.)
4. Half of the class may alternately play, while the other half either counts the pulsation, claps the rhythm, or concentrates on the fingering patterns.

As previously mentioned, the playing of simple wind instruments will facilitate the improvement of the skills in vocal music reading. To be of optimum value a variety of supplementary materials should be used. After the basic instruction book has been completed the teacher may utilize reading materials from the basic music series. Various benefits may accrue to the students when instrumental study is correlated with the singing program. Half the class may alternately play their instruments while the other half sings. Not only do the basic series provide a rich source of reading materials for the instrumentalist, but improved tonal security and vocal quality often result when the two activities are combined.

Orchestra bells, resonator bells

The orchestra bells (sometimes called melody bells) and resonator bells resemble a xylophone in the arrangement of the tone bars. All are played by striking with a small mallet. Some manufacturers of orchestra bells have painted the bars black and white to simulate the arrangement of the whole and half steps on the piano keyboard. The resonator bells are unique in that each tone bar may be removed from its position in the carrying case and played by individual children. Perhaps the easiest type of instrument to play is one involving a simple muscular movement. Therefore, instruments of this type, and the

---

[7] See procedure suggested on p. 183.

Melody Bells, and other mallet-played instruments, provide a desirable individual experience with tonal relationships.

resonator bells in particular, are highly suitable for use with young children. The range of musical experiences with such instruments, however, may vary from the simple to the more complex.

Beginning experiences with these instruments generally involve the playing of only one pitch, usually on the first beat of each measure as an accompaniment to a song. Rounds, sung in unison, are particularly adaptable for this purpose. For example:

Row, Row Your Boat

In the example, "Row, Row Your Boat" the symbol X indicates when the bar should be struck. In initial experiences, only one bar or bell should be struck and, in this case, C. Later, as children become more adept, they may play the actual pitch on the appropriate bell, indicated at the beginning of each measure. To provide a variety of materials, the teacher may wish to "arrange" certain songs by marking in the children's books, or in some cases by writing the song on the chalkboard so that all may see.[8]

The imaginative teacher will find many uses for these instruments. As children become more adept they may play entire melodies, usually as an accompaniment to class singing. For variety, the bells may be played on one phrase and the children may sing the next. For ear-training purposes, one child may play a short motive while another listens and then attempts to imitate what he heard.

In the intermediate grades the resonator bells may be used to supplement and clarify the teaching of vocal chording.[9] That is, the I, IV, and V chords in C Major may be written on the chalkboard and the bells for the pitches in these chords may be distributed to various children in the class. Each bell is imprinted with its respective pitch, and each child can identify his bell and then locate his pitch in one (or more) of the chords on the

[8] It is suggested that music written on the chalkboard for this purpose be in the public domain and not covered by copyright.

[9] See Chapter 8, p. 220, for a discussion of this procedure.

chalkboard. After each child understands the relationship of his pitch to the chord, he will strike his particular bell as the teacher points to the chord on the chalkboard. In this manner the resonator bells may be used as an accompaniment to singing or to provide tonal security for vocal chording. After children have had considerable experience in playing chords under the teacher's direction, they may be encouraged to listen carefully and decide where in the music their particular chord may be appropriately used. Special mallets are available for playing three bells simul-

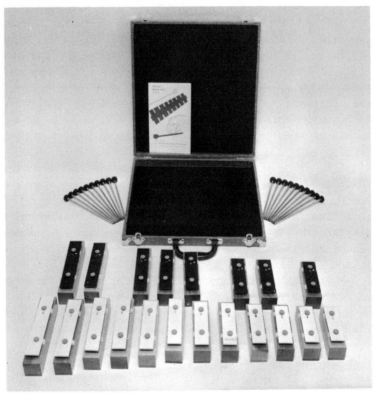

B. F. Kitching & Co., Inc.

A set of individual resonator bells, with carrying case and mallets. Bells may be arranged in case and played as a set of melody or orchestra bells, or they may be removed from the case for individual use.

taneously, and older children may be assigned a particular *chord*. They may select from the carrying case their tonal bars, and then determine those places in the music where their chord may be appropriately used. Experiences in which children have opportunity for making individual judgments may contribute substantially to their musical development.

Experience with chord and harmony instruments

Children need ample experience with harmony if they are to ultimately be successful in part-singing. Initial experiences involving careful listening will lead to the development of minds more receptive to theoretical explanations. The use of resonator bells in playing chords is an example of this latter type of experience. In addition, however, children need experiences with various other types of instruments which involve the use of harmony. These include principally the Autoharp, the Ukelele and the Guitar, and the Piano.

The autoharp

The simplest and easiest to play of the instruments of this type is the Autoharp. It is played by pressing a button producing the desired chord and simultaneously stroking the strings with a pick. Various types of picks may be used, each resulting in a different type of sound—a felt pick for soft, subdued tones and a plastic pick for louder, more brilliant sounds. In each bar there are slots cut in the damper felt which allow the desired strings in the chord to vibrate. For example, in the C Major chord, the slots are positioned above most of the C, E, and G strings. When the bar is depressed and the Autoharp stroked, these strings will vibrate while all the others are dampened. Autoharps are available in three basic models: the five bar, the twelve bar, and the fifteen bar. The five bar model is suitable for use with younger children and with simpler music where only a few chords are needed. With the twelve and fifteen bar autoharps, more chords are available and the player is less restricted in choice of chord and key. The twelve and fifteen bar models are recommended for use with intermediate grade children.[10]

Autoharps are an effective accompaniment for the singing of many songs. Certain songs in the basic series often include the letter names of the appropriate chords under the melodic line of the song. Generally, the player strokes the Autoharp on

Cincinnati Public Schools

Using the Autoharp in accompanying songs provides a desirable aural experience with harmony.

[10] For cardboard facsimiles of the Autoharp suitable for children to use at their desks while selected children play the actual instrument, see "12 Chord Practice Autoharp," available from National Autoharp Sales Company, P.O. Box 1120, University Station, Des Moines, Iowa 50311.

each beat of the music, sometimes on every other beat and occasionally on only the first beat of each measure, depending, of
course, upon the tempo and mood of the song. Chords are not
usually changed more often than once a measure. Simpler songs,
recommended for use with young children, may necessitate the
use of no more than two chords, and thus the instrument is
easily played by the beginning student.

The ukelele and the guitar

The fretted instruments, the ukelele and the guitar in
particular, have particular values for use in the music class. The
ukelele, although generally thought of as a recreational instrument only, has value in that it is relatively easy to play. Whenever possible, it is desirable for the school to purchase several
of these instruments for instructional purposes and so that
groups of students may alternately have the opportunity of accompanying the singing of selected songs. To illustrate the sim-
plicity of fingering, the positions for three basic chords are given
below. Each circle in the diagram indicates where the string
should be depressed and the number refers to the fingers in the
left hand that should be used.

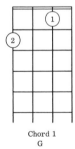

Chord 1
G

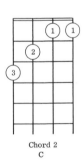

Chord 2
C

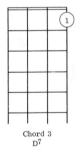

Chord 3
D⁷

After students have become familiar with the fingering
patterns for the above three chords, they should endeavor to
accompany the singing of certain songs. Successful early experiences will create interest and a desire to learn how to play other

chords. This information should be available to the student in the form of a basic instruction book.[11]

The guitar is more difficult to play than is the ukelele; however, experience with the latter is a desirable preparation for certain capable and interested students. It is desirable for classrooms to have available at least one guitar. It is also highly recommended that teachers develop some facility with this instrument and play accompaniments for certain selected songs. A degree of authenticity is created when the guitar is used to accompany certain types of folksongs—songs of the West and of Latin-America in particular.

The piano

The piano possesses a wide range of expressive possibilities and must be considered as more than simply a "chord or harmony" instrument. It is discussed here not only because of its educational values, but primarily because of its *relationship* to the total instrumental program. Some teachers make very broad and extensive use of the piano as a means of developing musicality in students. This is desirable whenever adequate class time exists and when the necessary number of instruments is available for class instruction. The piano, however, should be considered as an integral part of the instructional equipment and *all* children should have certain keyboard experiences which relate to the objectives of the overall program.

The piano may be used with very young children to facilitate the development of a feeling for tonal direction. The teacher may play various tones, beginning with the extreme ranges on the piano, and then ask the children if they were either high, low, or medium pitches. This activity is approached as a guessing

[11] Various instruction books are available through your local music store. In addition to finger charts some publications also include photos of actual hand positions. See, for example, Harry Reser, *Picture Chords for Standard Ukelele*, New York: Remick Music Corp., 1960.

game. The teacher may then ask certain children to come to the piano and play either a high, a low, or a medium pitch. In addition to "checking" the child's understanding of the concept, the remainder of the class may also be asked to respond as to the correctness of the child's playing. After the children have had some experience with this initial activity, the teacher may periodically play a song familiar to the children in various extremities of the keyboard and ask the class to identify the pitch level.[12]

A reasonable degree of familiarity with the keyboard is essential to a later understanding of scales and keys. The teacher may begin by having the entire class learn the names of the various keys on the keyboard and practice locating them. In explaining the grouping of the keys, the teacher may utilize a plastic keyboard, held in front of the class so that all may see. Attention should first be called to the combination of the black keys (in two's and three's) as a means of locating various pitches. After the class is told, for example, that the white key just to the left of the two black keys is C, certain children may be asked to come to the piano and play as many C's as they can find. Through orientation to the combinations of black keys the other tones in the diatonic scale may be likewise introduced.

Children should be taught the proper hand position for playing the piano. They should be asked to clench their fist and then open their hands only to the point where the tip of each finger may strike straight down on the keys. It is helpful if the fingers are thought of as pistons in an engine, *i.e.,* to do their best job they must move straight down without any sideways motion. Children should also be taught how to play the C scale and the principle of tucking the thumb *under* (fourth scale step) on the ascending scale and bringing the third finger *over* (third scale step) on the descending scale. Children should be encouraged to experiment on their pianos at home and to endeavor to "pick out" the melodies of familiar tunes.

Whenever one to three different tone bars of the resonator

12 See Chapter 2, pp. 34-37, for a discussion of related activities.

bells are used for accompanying singing, the same pitches may also be played by one or two children at the piano. Also, when in the intermediate grades children have learned vocal chording and the playing of chords on the resonator bells, they should also be taught to play the I, IV and V chords at the piano. These chords may be used separately as an accompaniment to singing or may be combined with the other instruments. Learning to play these three chords on the piano serves to reinforce the concepts learned through other media, as well as laying a foundation for future learning experiences with the piano. With only this minimal background in piano, students might experiment on their pianos at home and endeavor to create original tunes. Children can become fascinated by the combinations of chords that they can devise, and as a result often develop a desire to notate their "masterpieces" for posterity. When students possess this desire they are usually more receptive to learning the mechanics of music notation.

Band and orchestral instruments

Learning to play a band or an orchestral instrument can make a very significant contribution to children's musical development. While instruction in these instruments, usually begun in the fourth grade, is the responsibility of the special music teacher, the classroom teacher can contribute to this aspect of the music program in varied ways. He may periodically ask the children to bring their instruments to class and to play selections of their own choice for each other. Utilizing a small selected instrumental ensemble as an accompaniment for group singing may prove an interesting experience. Some of the basic music series include instrumental parts for various instruments. When such materials are not available, classroom teachers may seek advice in the arranging of instrumental parts from the special instrumental teachers. In general, children will benefit whenever the classroom teacher exhibits interest in individual progress.

Topics for discussion

1. Discuss the various merits and advantages of having children construct their own simple rhythm instruments, as opposed to having them play only factory-made ones.

2. What advantages and disadvantages exist in asking students to purchase their own simple wind instruments, as opposed to using school owned instruments? What procedures should the teacher follow in asking students to purchase instruments?

3. Discuss the various combinations of instruments that may be used for accompanying singing. What factors should determine one's choice of certain instruments?

4. Discuss the advantages and disadvantages of class instrumental instruction as opposed to individual instruction. Is there a place for both?

5. Discuss the factor of *readiness* as it relates to the appropriate time for the introduction of certain types of instruments.

Suggestions for further study

ELLIOTT, Raymond. *Teaching Music: Methods and Materials for the Elementary Schools.* Columbus, Ohio: Merrill, 1960, Ch. 7.

ELLISON, Alfred. *Music With Children.* McGraw-Hill, New York: 1959, Chs. 5 & 6.

MANDELL, Muriel and WOOD, Robert E. *Make Your Own Musical Instruments.* New York: Sterling Publishing Company, 1957.

MASON, Bernard S. *Drums, Tomtoms, and Rattles.* New York: Barnes, 1938.

130   **Music in childhood education**

MORALES, Humbert. *Latin American Rhythm Instruments*. New York:
H. Adler Publishers Corp., 1954.

NYE, Robert E. and NYE, Vernice T. *Music in the Elementary School,*
2nd ed. Englewood Cliffs, N.J.: Prentice-Hall, 1964, Ch. 5.

PACE, Robert. *Piano for Classroom Music*. Englewood Cliffs, N.J.:
Prentice-Hall, 1956.

SWANSON, Bessie R. *Music in the Education of Children,* 2nd ed. Belmont, Calif.: Wadsworth, 1964, Chs. 4 & 5.

Suggested materials

BECKMAN, Frederick. *Clasroom Method for Melody Flute*. Laurel,
Maryland: Melody Flute Company, 1952.

BRADFORD, Margaret, and PARKER, Elizabeth. *How to Play the Recorder,*
Books I and II. New York: G. Schirmer, Inc., 1938.

DAVIS, Henry W. *Tonette Tuner and Technic*. Chicago: Rubank, Inc.,
1941.

EARLE, Frederick. *Music-time for Flutophone and Other Pre-Band Instruments*. Cleveland: Trophy Products Company, 1961.

GOLDING, Sally, LONSTEIN, Eugene, and Ross, Jerrold. *Melodies for
Music Makers*. 2nd Edition, revised. Far Rockaway, N.Y.: Carl Van
Roy Company, 1964 (good for correlation with singing and other
activities).

GOODYEAR, Stephen. *The New-Recorder Tutor,* Books I and II. New
York: Mills Music, Inc., 1956, 1957.

LANAHAN, Walter D. *Melody Method for the Recorder*. Revised Edition. Laurel, Maryland: Melody Flute Company, 1956.

PRIESTLY, Edmund, and FOWLER, Fred. *The School Recorder,* Books 1
and 2. London: E. J. Arnold & Son Limited Leeds, 1962 (available
through Hargail Music Press, N.Y.).

TRAPP FAMILY SINGERS. *Enjoy Your Recorder*. Sharon, Conn.: Magna-
music Distributors, Inc., 1954.

VAN PELT, Merrill B., and RUDDICK, J. Leon. *Flutophone Classroom Method*. Revised Edition. Cleveland: Trophy Products Company, 1948.

WEBER, Fred. *Pre-Instrument Method*. Rockville Centre, L.I., N.Y., Belwin, Inc., 1950.

Films

The Autoharp (Johnson Hunt Productions, 6509 De Longpre Ave., Hollywood, Calif.), 1955, b&w, 19 min. Col.

Keyboard Experiences In Classroom Music (American Music Conference, 332 South Michigan Ave., Chicago, Ill. 60604), 1957, b&w, 23 min. Col.

Rhythm and Percussion (Encyclopaedia Britannica Films, 1150 Wilmette Ave., Wilmette, Ill.), 1950, b&w, 12 min. Elem./Col.

6 Creative activities

What are creative activities? To some persons the term *creative* means only the development of something new and original. According to this viewpoint, which has long been held, it would not be a completely creative act to merely perform music written by someone else. However, around 1925, a new concept appeared which implies that all learning is creative with reference to the learner. The thought implicit in this belief is that the learner himself must fully comprehend ideas, concepts, and relationships so that they are something more than merely words or symbols and thus become a part of his total experience. Since no one else can ever do this for him, such learning can be said to be "created" by the learner. A key word which aptly describes this process is "discovery"; for a child to discover a new fact or relationship necessitates insight and understanding which must come from, or be "created" within, the individual.[1] Another related term is *re-creative*, often used in connection with the traditional viewpoint of creativity. Persons using this term would usually take the position that while musical performance is not a new creative act, the performer

[1] For two points of view in regard to the term, "creative," the following sources are suggested for further reading: William H. Burton, *The Guidance of Learning Activities*, Third Edition, New York: Appleton-Century-Crofts, 1962, Chapter 16, and James L. Mursell, *Music Education: Principles and Programs*, New York: Silver-Burdett and Company, 1956.

must at least possess a certain degree of insight and musical understanding if the music is to be interpreted in a musicianly manner.

What are the implications of this new viewpoint of creativity for the teaching of music? In singing a song or playing an instrument a creative approach necessitates that the music be meaningful to the performer and that he be able to perform it in a manner satisfactory to himself. Musical artistry is dependent upon the degree of musical insight the performer possesses; creativity, however, is not dependent upon an arbitrary or fixed level of musical proficiency and insight. For example, a second grade student who possesses a reasonable understanding of the text and mood of a song and the relationship between the words and the music, and who is able to relate his past experiences to this song, is likely to perform or "re-create" it in a highly satisfactory manner. This can be a truly creative act, commensurate with the degree of insight which the child possesses. Furthermore, an experienced adult who possesses a knowledge of the stylistic aspects of the music, and who is sensitive to all the necessary subtle nuances, will be less likely to perform in an unmusical and mechanical manner. The insight leading to a creative performance must come from within the individual and cannot be simply imposed upon a person or group. This does not mean, however, that teachers cannot facilitate the development of insight, for this is one of their primary functions.

The teacher's point of departure, however, should not be, "Shall I plan for a creative work, a re-creative act, or simply a discovery?" but rather, "What can I do to provide meaningful learning experiences for the class?" The teacher can begin by providing a classroom atmosphere conducive to effective learning and by exploring with the students all information that will contribute to improved performance. This approach to teaching should permeate all music activities, whether they be singing, playing, rhythmic activities, or listening.

While some educators are critical of the use of the term "creative" to describe these activities, most will admit that this particular philosophy has contributed to the development of more desirable learning situations. Actually, it is less important whether the teacher uses the word "creative," "re-creative," or "discovery" in connection with music activities, and more important what he actually does in the classroom in terms of providing meaningful learning experiences. The teacher who is really dynamic and imaginative in the teaching of music will most certainly provide the children with an ideal background for those experiences which result in the "creation" of the completely new and original.

The scope of creative activity

Some persons are inclined to think only of composing music as a truly creative endeavor. Actually, many varied possibilities for a creative approach to teaching exist in each avenue of musical experience. While discussed in detail in other chapters, this information is summarized here to point up the scope and interrelatedness of creative activities.

In rhythmic activities, emphasis is placed upon the expression of various thoughts and ideas through bodily movement. Activities ranging from simple movements, such as "swaying like a tree" or "marching like a soldier," to the complete dramatization of a song or recorded selection are all integral parts of the creative approach to the teaching of music.

The actual making of rhythm band instruments is a creative activity of considerable value to children. More important, however, is the opportunity for the development of musical understanding and discrimination that results when children are provided opportunity for creating rhythm orchestrations and actually notating them. The selection of various types and combinations of instruments for use in accompanying the singing of songs is also a highly beneficial experience, one which involves the making of many judgments.

Listening to music creatively may occur when children are led to a higher level of appreciation through an understanding of all the aspects of music that contribute to its existence as an expressive art. Listening lessons on such topics as tempo, dynamics, mood, imagery, styles of articulation, components of music, and musical form may all contribute to the development of musical awareness and insight.

An important aspect of creativity in singing is song interpretation. As opposed to simply a teacher-imposed interpretation, the children should be led through carefully planned experiences (usually involving ample class discussion) to a full realization of the import of the expressive aspects of the text and the music. Through class discussion children may be encouraged to think about and express their opinions on textual meanings, the proper tempo and dynamics, or the general interpretation of the song. Harmonizing "by ear" a second part to a familiar song and learning how to notate this additional part is a creative experience leading to a clearer understanding of music notation and an increased skill in both music reading and part-singing.

Children should also have ample experience in singing their thoughts and feelings, singing questions and answers, creating new words to familiar songs, and in composing songs. In addition, they should have experience with such related activities as creating stories, chants and poems, and with choral speaking, where a study is made of the meter and rhythm of poetry and of the subtle nuances of words. Approaches to the teaching of these types of activities are discussed in the following sections of this chapter.

Creating music

Creating songs as a group or individual endeavor has a number of values. Such activities facilitate the development of the imagination and individual resourcefulness, and they contribute to the development of *esprit de corps* within a class. The end product becomes "our song." Perhaps most important is that the activity increases the children's insight into the inner workings of music; an increased understanding is gained of how a song comes into being, how the words are related to the melody, and of the subtle nuances which exist in a creative product. In addition, the class gains an appreciation of the efforts that others have made in the creative process. Some of these important understandings can be gained in no other way than through the experience of actually creating a song.

Creating the proper classroom atmosphere

It is the teacher's responsibility to develop and maintain an atmosphere in the classroom that is conducive to creative work. Proper heating, ventilation, and lighting should, of course, be maintained. A properly ventilated room is essential to the maintenance of alert minds, and window shades may need periodic adjustment to avoid glare. Classrooms should have an adequate number of facilities for displaying student work, such as bulletin boards, cases, and tables. When these facilities are properly utilized with displays of on-going class work, the atmosphere in the classroom is generally more conducive to creative work in related fields.

Students in the classroom should feel reasonably secure within themselves if creative work is to be achieved. The teacher can contribute in many ways to the development of this security, but specifically, he can help each child to discover his own particular strengths. To do so he should utilize a type of pupil-teacher planning that enables each child to make his own unique contribution to the class.[2]

The teacher should patiently guide each child to the development of his maximum capabilities. Criticism of a biting, sarcastic nature is inexcusable and should never occur, as it will simply cause a child to withdraw further into himself. Under such circumstances, creativity is likely to be completely stifled.

---

[2] For specific suggestions in regard to teacher-pupil planning, see *Principles of Modern Education*, Ralph L. Pounds and Robert L. Garretson, New York: Macmillan and Company, 1962, pp. 267-274.

As the children mature, they may be led gradually into the process of analyzing their creative work, and from this experience they will profit and re-direct their energies towards increased improvement of skills and understandings. In the initial stages of creative work, however, it is generally best to avoid criticism. The emphasis at this stage should be upon self-expression, not the level of quality of the ultimate musical product.

Initial creative experiences

If skills in creating music are to be ultimately achieved, then the teacher should begin the creative process early. This creative process should be an outgrowth of the on-going class activity. With this thought in mind, the teacher should periodically encourage the children to sing their thoughts rather than speak them. If children are enthusiastic about their class work and have something they would like to express about the topic of study, then this type of creative expression is quite readily achieved.

Questions and answers

If an adequate foundation has been laid for expressing one's thoughts through song, and when this expression is natural, spontaneous, and enjoyable, then the teacher may utilize musical questions and answers as a part of the class work. In other words, the teacher sings a question and the designated pupil responds in any way he feels is most appropriate. For this procedure to be effective, the answers to the questions must be readily understood by the children. To determine this factor the teacher may in some cases ask the question verbally, and then after the child has responded, repeat the question by singing it. The on-going class activity, especially when it centers about the field of social studies, offers ample opportunity for musical questions and answers. This type of activity may be begun in the first grade and continued throughout the intermediate grades by adjusting the word content of the questions and by singing more intricate musical questions. In the initial stages, the questions should be relatively short and phrased in such a manner as to necessitate a simple and rather direct answer. Following are some typical questions that could be sung and some probable answers.

As the children grow in their skill of answering musical questions, the teacher may devise questions that necessitate a slightly more elaborate and extended answer. Two possible questions and answers growing out of a unit on "Our Community" are as follows:

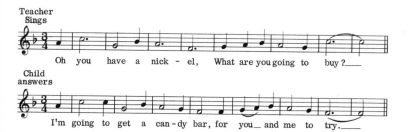

The imaginative teacher will, in the normal course of a teaching unit, discover many topics suitable for musical questions. Following are some examples of questions and probable answers that might be utilized with units of study on particular grade levels.

Unit topic: Neighborhood Helpers (grades 1-2)
1. Who helps us cross the street?
   The policeman helps us cross the street.
2. Who wears a big red hat?
   The fireman wears a big red hat.
3. Who helps us when we're sick?
   The doctor helps us when we're sick.

Unit topic: Indians (grade 3)
1. Where do Indians live?
   They live in many places.
2. How do they get their food?
   They go hunting in the forest.
3. Do Indians like to dance?
   Yes, Indians like to dance.

Unit topic: Mexico (grade 4)
1. Who is Juanita?
   Juanita is a little girl.
2. Where does Juanita live?
   Juanita lives in Mexico
3. How can we get to Juanita's home?
   We can ride a donkey to Juanita's home.

Creating new verses

Creating new or additional verses to a familiar song is an activity which may be utilized on all grade levels beginning in about the second or the third grade, depending upon the children's background and development. Following is a generalized procedure which is recommended for this activity:

1. Ask the class to think of words and ideas they are reminded of as they sing a particular familiar song.
2. Write the list of suggested words on the chalkboard.
3. Ask the students to think of complete sentences or phrases (using the list of words or related ideas) that will fit with the first phrase of the song.
4. Write the suggestions of the class on the chalkboard. (If more than one suggestion, let the class select the line or phrase they like best.)
5. Repeat the process for the remaining phrases of the song (steps 3 and 4).

Children enjoy creating new words to songs when the topic is within the realm of their own experiences. Following is an additional verse which one third grade class created for the song "America, the Beautiful." [3]

> George Washington was President in seventeen eighty-nine,
> He helped design our country's flag, our symbol for all time.
> Oh, Betsy Ross made our first flag, with stars and stripes so new,
> She stitched our banner carefully, the red, the white, and blue.

[3] Written by a third grade class at Losantiville School, Cincinnati, Ohio; Mrs. Natalie Skurow, teacher.

Children are capable of devising highly unique and clever additional verses to familiar songs. As in the previous example, the new verses will grow out of, and elaborate upon, the already familiar existing verses. In other cases, children will simply use a favorite tune and devise verses entirely unrelated to the existing text.

The following verse, as well as the title, was devised by a fifth-grade class as part of a school project called "Clean Up Week," held in both the spring and fall.[4]

Tune: "Clementine" Title: "The Can Can"

Pick up paper,
On the school ground,
Put it in the nearest can.
It will soon become a habit,
To use the trash can.
This is a rule,
Don't break it,
Obey it all the time.
It will soon become a habit
To use the trash can.

Children often enjoy creating verses on their own. One fourth grade student, after encouragement from his teacher, created the following, which was an outgrowth of a unit of study on library resource materials.

Tune: "Pepsi-Cola Hits the Spot"

The Encyclopedia's a good, good book!
One glance at first was all we took,
Now we definitely do agree,
The Encyclopedia's for you and me!

[4] Written by fifth grade students at Pleasant Ridge Elementary School, Cincinnati, Ohio: Miss Sara McSpadden, teacher.

In addition to encouraging individual creative efforts, the teacher will often find it desirable to arrange for children to work either in small groups or in pairs. The following verse, by two second grade children, was written during the last week of school. It reflects the children's thoughts and reveals their unique sense of humor.[5]

Tune: "I've Been Workin' on the Railroad"

> I've been workin' in the classroom,
> All the live-long day.
> I've been workin' in the classroom,
> Just to pass this term away.
> Can't you hear the parents singing,
> "Teacher, don't blow your top.
> Hang on a little bit longer,
> It's June and school will stop!"
>
> Children, go home; Children, go home;
> Children, go home, Hooray! Hooray!
> Children, go home; Children, go home;
> Children, go home, Hooray!
>
> No one's in the classroom with teacher,
> No one's in the classroom, you see.
> No one's in the classroom with teacher,
> No one's here but me!

Creating additional words to a song is an activity suitable for any age level. Even classroom teachers gain increased insight into the creative process when they participate in this activity. Some of the results are quite unique.

Tune: "I've Been Workin' on the Railroad"

> The trains were running on the track,
> The smoke was pouring out.

[5] Written by second grade children at the Westwood Primary School, Cincinnati, Ohio; Mrs. Joy Roof, teacher.

The wheels were going clickety-clack,
The conductor gave a shout.
I heard the whistle moaning sadly,
The train was not on time.
Won't you throw the switches quickly?
Dinah, get off this line!

Tune: "Home on the Range"

When the shadows at night gather 'round the fire bright,
And the mountains reflect the sun's glow.
When the sky hangs her stars to hear the guitars,
I sing of my home long ago.
Boots, saddles, and spurs are all that a cowboy does own,
But I never would trade great nature's parade,
For all of the jobs ever known.

Tune: "Clementine"

Swimming down the Colorado,
Blowing bubbles all the way,
Caught a brook trout in my tonsil,
Now I'm going the other way."

Chorus: "Oh, my darling, etc."

Composing songs

The creation of songs is generally more successful when composing the poem and the music is all one unified creative act growing out of a topic in which there is a high degree of motivation. The following generalized procedure is recommended for composing songs. If, however, the teacher wishes to utilize a poem written by someone other than the class, then step one through five would be omitted. In this case, it is essential that motivation be provided through adequate discussion of the poem prior to setting it to music.

1. Motivation is important. A topic or idea growing out of a unit of work, a specific holiday, or special event, is

more likely to provide the motivation necessary for successful completion of a creative act than teacher selected and imposed ideas.

2. Question the children. For example, "What events happen in the fall of the year that you particularly enjoy?" Write list of topics on the chalkboard: [6]

> football games
> falling leaves
> Halloween

3. Let the class select the topic they would prefer to discuss further.

4. If, for example, the topic Halloween is chosen by the group, the teacher might ask the question, "What are some ideas that come to your mind when you think of Halloween?" Place list of ideas on chalkboard in columns:

candy	bats	skeletons
masquerades	witches	devils
parties	black cats	costumes
spooks	goblins	fairies
pumpkins	ghosts	graveyards

5. Suggest to the class that, with the preceding list of words in mind, they think of some complete ideas or sentences.
   a. Call on four or five students to recite their ideas.
   b. Let the class vote and select the idea they like best. Then write it on the chalkboard.
   c. Repeat procedure until a short poem of four lines has been developed.

6. Develop a feeling for accent.
   a. Ask the class to read the poem aloud in unison.
   b. Read again and accent the important words.

[6] The list of topics and words listed here were suggested by a fourth grade class approximately one week before Halloween.

    c. Underline the important words on the chalkboard
    and place a vertical line before the accented words.

7. Determine the mood of the poem. Ask the question,
"Is the poem happy and carefree, or sombre and scary?"
In a natural sequence of events, this step usually is de-
termined rather quickly.

8. Determine the mode. The teacher should play major
and minor chords and scales on the piano. Let the class
vote and select the mode (either major or minor) which
they feel best fits the mood of the poem.

Cincinnati Public Schools

**Topics of current interest to children provide excellent motivation for the
creating of songs.**

9. Instruct the children to think of appropriate melodies to go with the first line of the poem.
   a. Request the entire class to sing together silently.
   b. Ask four or five students to sing their melodies for the class.
   c. The class should then vote and select the melody they like best.
   d. The teacher should notate the appropriate syllables on the chalkboard under the words.
   e. Repeat procedure for the other lines of the poem. (Later, at his convenience, the teacher may notate the song on the chalkboard and/or on manuscript paper. If the students have a reasonable degree of understanding of notation, they may assist the teacher in this process.)

10. Duplicate copies of the song in order that the children may have a record of their cooperative group achievement.

11. Utilize the song as a part of the children's regular song repertoire.

The following two songs, "Lightning" and "Birthdays," were written by third grade children and illustrate the use of their *own* topics, imagery and vocabulary.

Lightning [7]

Light-ning is our ham-ster, as soft as he can be, He
runs and scam-pers all a - round, and will not come to me.

[7] This song was written by third grade children at the Demonstration School, University of Wisconsin at Milwaukee; Dr. Nancy Nunnally, teacher.

Birthdays [8]

A birth - day is a hap - py day, It
To - day is (Johnnie's) birth - day, And

..comes but once a year.____ It makes us want to
he is (eight) years old.____ We hope you'll have a

cel - e - brate, It makes us want to cheer.____
hap - py day, And a year as good as gold.____

Seasons of the year, or specific holidays, may provide the motivation necessary for creative work. The song "Autumn Days," written by a fifth grade class, grew out of a discussion of "events we enjoy in the autumn."

Autumn Days [9]

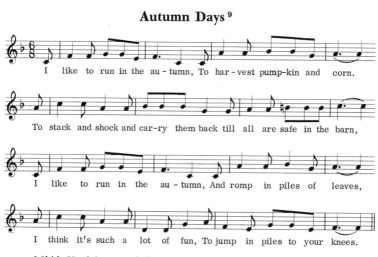

I like to run in the au - tumn, To har - vest pump-kin and corn.

To stack and shock and car-ry them back till all are safe in the barn,

I like to run in the au - tumn, And romp in piles of leaves,

I think it's such a lot of fun, To jump in piles to your knees.

[8] *Ibid.* Used by permission.

[9] This song was written by fifth grade children at Glendale School, Cincinnati, Ohio; Miss Grace Eilert, teacher.

Units of study, organized around the social studies, provide children with a necessary pool of thoughts and ideas, which can be drawn upon for the creating of songs. The song "Annie Oakley" grew out of a fifth grade unit on "Ohio—Our State."

Annie Oakley [10]

1. There was a maid in our great state, In shoot - ing she was sure - ly great, she could shoot a quail right thro' the head, And when they fell, they were sure - ly dead.

2. Now Green-ville O - hi - o, she claimed as her home, In woods north of there, she'd al - ways roam. Yes An - nie Oak-ley that was her name, As cham - pion "crack shot" she made her fame.

3. In a contest with Butler she easily won, this made a match in more ways than one. In the wild west show of Buffalo Bill, Annie Oakley continued to prove her skill.

4. In remembering names of Ohio's great,
Please remember this champion of our state. (Repeat)

The Carl Orff approach

Carl Orff is considered one of Germany's foremost composers, and such works as his *Carmina Burana, Catulli Carmina,* and *Antigonæ,* for example, are well-known to the musical world. He has become, in recent years, equally well-known for his work in music education. The first edition of his *Schulwerk* appeared in 1930, but was written for an older age group. In 1948, Bavarian Radio, intrigued after hearing an out-of-print recording of his earlier work, asked Orff to write music "along

[10] *Ibid.* Used by permission.

these lines" that children would be able to play for a series of broadcasts. The present edition of *Schulwerk*, then, grew out of this effort and from the experience of working with children in preparing these and subsequent programs.[11]

The basic purpose underlying the Orff approach is "the development of a child's creative faculty which manifests itself in the ability to improvise." [12] Orff's beginning point is rhythm, taught initially through speech patterns which the child can readily comprehend. Through this approach a clearer understanding of tonal contrast, dynamics, phrasing, and note values is developed.[13] Clapping, knee-slapping (patschen), stamping, finger snapping, and percussion instruments are all used as a means of achieving a clearer perception of rhythm.

Orff has designed a complete set of instruments, which take into consideration the physical limitations of children. These are the Glockenspiel (soprano and alto), the Metalophone (soprano and alto), the Xylophone (soprano, alto, and bass), the Bordun (a two-stringed instrument), Timpani (small, medium, and large in size), a Bass drum, small drums, woodblock, cymbals, triangle, and jingles or shells (small sleigh bells). Other instruments used are the Recorder and tuned water glasses.

Melodic experiences begin with the falling minor third, because of children's familiarity with the interval. The range is gradually widened to include the pentatonic (five-tone) scale (C,D,E,G,A), which Orff feels is well-suited for children's early experiences with music.[14] (The first volume of *Music for Children* is pentatonic, however, the subsequent volumes deal with major and minor.)

[11] Carl Orff (translated by Arnold Walter), "The Schulwerk—Its Origin and Aims," *Music Educators Journal,* Volume 49, No. 5, April-May, 1963, pp. 69-74.

[12] Carl Orff and Gunild Keetman, *Music for Children, Book I, Pentatonic,* Mainz, Germany: B. Schott's Söhne, 1956, p. iv.

[13] Doreen Hall, *Teacher's Manual, Music for Children,* Mainz, Germany: B. Schott's Söhne, 1960, pp. 6, 13-19. For other examples of speech patterns, see *Book I, Pentatonic,* pp. 66-70.

[14] This is the most common form of the pentatonic scale; it follows the same scheme as that of the black keys on the piano (beginning on F#), *i.e.,* whole step, whole step, minor third, and whole step.

Echo clapping, in which the teacher claps a one or two measure rhythmic pattern which is immediately imitated by the children, appropriately leads into echo playing on the Xylophone and Glockenspiel. The C, D, and A pitches are removed from the instruments and the pitches G and E are used initially, thus simplifying the echo response of the child. Later the A pitch is added. These three pitches comprise the familiar sound of the children's chant:

Eventually, after the children have had appropriate experiences, all five tones in the pentatonic scale are used.

Rhythmic canon, a form of simple polyphony in which one group imitates the patterns begun by another group (usually after one measure), is another device used to develop children's musicality. They grow out of experiences with echo clapping and speech canons. (For specific teaching suggestions, see pp. 22-23 in the *Teacher's Manual* by Doreen Hall.) Melodic canon grows out of experiences with echo playing. Following is an example of a simple melodic canon.[15]

Prior to playing canons on instruments, it is suggested that children have ample experience in singing vocal canons. (For other examples of rhythmic and melodic canons, see pp. 82-83 in *Book I Pentatonic*.)

Rhythmic phrase building, in which rhythmic phrases are clapped by the teacher and then continued and concluded by the children in various ways, is considered as the first step toward improvisation. For example: [16]

[15] Carl Orff and Gunild Keetman, *Music for Children, Book I, Pentatonic,* Mainz, Germany: B. Schott's Söhne, 1956, p. 83. Used by permission of Associated Music Publishers, Inc., New York.

Teacher claps   Possible children's responses

Each child should have ample opportunity to complete the phrases begun by the teacher, and should be encouraged to create his own unique responses. This experience, of course, leads into melodic phrase building, in which the teacher plays a melodic pattern which is then continued and concluded by the child. For the initial experiences it is desirable to use only the tones E, G, and A, thus simplifying the response of the child. For example: [17]

Teacher plays   Children's responses

16 *Ibid.,* p. 84. Used by permission.
17 *Ibid.,* p. 85. Used by permission.

As the child progresses in his ability to complete phrases other tones may be added and the phrases may be lengthened to eight and even sixteen measures.

Ostinato (a figure repeated throughout a composition) is used as an accompaniment for improvisation. Rhythmic ostinati may involve combinations of clapping, patschen, finger snapping, and various percussion instruments. (For examples, see pp. 71-78, *Book I Pentatonic.*) The Glockenspiel, Metalophone, Xylophone, Timpani, and Gamba are used in playing melodic ostinati. Melodic accompaniments begin with the Bordun, or open fifth. Moving Borduns may be created by changing either or both the notes (melodically—by steps or leaps, or rhythmically), thus developing the ostinato figure. Various ostinati are used, of which the following are only a few of the many possibilities.[18]

The rondo is considered to be the best form for improvisation. In the rhythmic rondo the teacher and the class clap and stamp the theme, with individual children improvising the contrasting sections.[19] This activity quite naturally leads into the use of the melodic rondo, in which the same general approach is used, but with instruments rather than clapping. Until the children comprehend the form, and develop their ability to improvise, the melodic rondo may be taught as a piece with inter-

18 *Ibid.* Used by permission.
19 For a discussion of the rondo form see p. 86.

ludes played by individuals. (For examples of rhythmic and melodic rondos, see pp. 86-90 in *Book I Pentatonic*.)

The above discussion highlights only some of the principal ideas in the Orff approach. For those persons interested in developing a broader understanding of these methods, the following publications are recommended.

> Orff, Carl (translated by Arnold Walter), "The Schulwerk —Its Origin and Aims," *Music Educators Journal*, Volume 49, No. 5, April-May, 1963, pp. 69-74. (Also in *The Canadian Music Educator*, October-November, 1962.)
>
> Orff, Carl, and Gunild Keetman, *Music for Children* (English adaptation by Doreen Hall and Arnold Walter). Mainz, Germany: B. Schott's Söhne (available from Associated Music Publishers, Inc., One W. 47th St., New York, N. Y. 10036).
>
>> Includes "Nursery Rhymes and Songs," "I Pentatonic," "II Major: Bordun," "III Major: Triads," "IV Minor: Bordun," "V Minor: Triads."
>
> Hall, Doreen, *Music for Children, Teacher's Manual*. Mainz, Germany: B. Schott's Söhne, 1960 (available from Associated Music Publishers).
>
> Film: *Music for Children*. (available from Contemporary Films, 267 West 25th St., New York, N. Y. 10001).
>
> Recording: *Music for Children*. Angel 3582.
> (available through your local music store).
>
> For sources of the Orff-designed instruments, see the Appendix, pp. 257-58.

Increasing interest is being shown in the Orff approach by music educators throughout America. Various workshops are held periodically, usually on college and university campuses, to clarify this approach. For the music educator who wishes to gain more knowledge of the Orff method, attendance at one of these workshops is highly recommended.

Related activities contributing to creativity in music

Creativity should not be limited to the music program, but should permeate all the curricular areas. The area of language arts is a particularly fertile field for utilizing a creative approach. The classroom teacher, whose responsibility it is to implement such a program, will find that a creative approach is essential to the accomplishment of objectives in this field and that it contributes substantially to creativeness in various related areas.

Creating stories, chants, and poems

The creating of stories, chants, and poems is a valuable means by which self-expression through language may be taught. Stories may be either oral or written. A good beginning point is the use of "open-ended" stories, in which the teacher relates the first part of the story and the children complete it. Music recordings may be played to stimulate imagery and the class may be asked to either write or express orally their feelings and impressions. Educational silent films are also available for the express purpose of stimulating creative thought.[20] Each member of the class, after viewing the film, may write his own interpretation of it. Field trips to various noteworthy locations in the community are a valuable means of broadening classroom experiences and making them more meaningful. They also provide a common experience for the entire class and an additional basis for oral and written expression.

Chants of various types seem to be a natural part of children's play and a form of expression which they all enjoy. Most

20 See, for example, the film, *The Hunter and the Forest* by Arne Sucksdorff, distributed by Encyclopaedia Britannica Films, Wilmette, Ill.

children have a considerable repertoire of chants which they use, for example, for rope-jumping. It is suggested that teachers ask the children to share these chants with each other in the class. The question, "How do the chants help your rope-jumping?" should be posed. After some discussion of this topic, the class should be encouraged to create additional chants for variety and enjoyment. Variations of existing chants or entirely new ones may be shared with the class from time to time.

Prior to this the teacher will want to observe children chanting on the playground and perhaps notate some of the verses which they hear. It should, of course, be understood that these chants are a part of the children's sub-culture and some of their beliefs and attitudes are obtained through them. Children are likely to sometimes develop their own variations of chants. Compare the following chants with the "renditions" in your community.

Had a little monkey, its name was Tiny Tim,
I put him in the bathtub to teach him how to swim.
He drank up all the water and he ate up all the soap,
And he died last night with a bubble in his throat.

In came the doctor, in came the nurse,
In came the lady with the alligator purse.
Out went the doctor, out went the nurse,
Out went the lady with the alligator purse.

Not last night, but the night before,
Twenty-four robbers came knockin' at my door.
Went down stairs to let them in,
They hit me over the head with a rollin' pin.

Went upstairs to get my gun,
Shot those robbers one by one.
How many robbers did I shoot?
One, two, three, etc. (to 24).

Blue bells and cockle shells,
Eevy, Ivy, over.

Here comes the teacher with a big black stick,
Better get out your arithmetic!

One and one are two, two and two are four.
Now its time for spelling.
C-A-T spells cat, R-A-T spells rat.
Now its time to spell your name on one foot.
Capital N,A,N,C,Y.

Blondie and Dagwood went downtown,
Blondie bought an evening gown.
Dagwood bought a pair of shoes,
Cookie read the evening news.

This is what the paper read.
Close your eyes and count to ten,
And if you miss you take an end.
One, two, three, etc.

Children enjoy the rhyme and rhythm of poetry and after some experience with choral speaking (discussed in the following section), the class should be encouraged to write original poems. As a group or class endeavor, the same general procedures as presented in steps 1-5 for creating new verses (Ch. 6, p. 140) may be utilized. Individual students also should be encouraged to create poems on topics in which they are highly interested.

Choral speaking

Choral speaking is utilized by many classroom teachers as a means of fulfilling certain of the objectives of the language arts program. Choral speaking has numerous values that also contribute substantially to the objectives of the music program as well. While choral speaking is not within the realm of responsibility of music teachers, they should nevertheless understand fully the relationship between this activity and music and should encourage its inclusion in the curriculum whenever possible.

Children display a natural liking for rhyme and rhythm. Through choral speaking, they develop an increased awareness of rhyming words and a feeling for meter (measured rhythm).[21] Choral speaking, in general, assists children in developing a sensitivity to beauty in thought, word, and tone. It increases the child's vocabulary, his understanding of the dramatic qualities of words, and improves habits of speech such as enunciation and pronunciation.

An awareness of nuances in music—subtle or delicate graduations in musical expression, either in tone, tempo, color, or volume—is basic to an artistic musical performance. Choral speaking provides children insight into this important aspect of music interpretation, as well as providing a background for understanding the relationship between words, and rhythm, tempo, tone quality, and phrasing.

For the purpose of achieving tonal contrast in choral speaking the voices of children are grouped in various ways. In the primary grades the voices of younger children are often uniformly high. Differences in pitch level are not distinct enough to warrant classifying the voices into such categories as high, medium, and low. Therefore, a desirable procedure is to divide the class into two groups—either boys and girls or left and right sides of the room. Reciting certain phrases in unison, and utilizing solo voices on others, provides a further means of achieving tonal variety with this age group.

The following poems illustrate the division of voices appropriate to the primary grades.[22]

The Little Stone
by Ethel Mahler

Boys: How quiet is the little stone
Just sitting there all day.
Girls: It has no arms or legs
To run about and play.
All: Sometimes I wish I were a stone
When I am tired and sit alone.

[21] Finger plays for young children can be another way of expressing rhythm and getting experience in choral speaking.

[22] From *Verse Choir in the Elementary School*, Clifford E. Barton, Darien, Conn.: Educational Publishing Corporation, 1954. Used by permission.

The Fly and the Elephant
by Adelyn Richards

All: The elephant teased,
Solo boy: "Why, you are so small
That really, a fly
Means nothing at all!"
Solo girl: "Your feet,"
All: Said the fly
Solo girl: "Cover half of the lawn,
But how many ceilings
Have they walked on?"

In the intermediate grades greater variety and more subtle tonal differences may be achieved by classifying the students' voices into three categories—high, medium, and low. Continued and refined use of unison speaking and solo voices is also recommended. The following are suggested steps for classifying students' voices.

1. Write the three categories (high, medium, and low) on the chalkboard.
2. Ask each child to read aloud a short poem, selected previously by the teacher.
3. Let the class determine if each person's voice sounds high, low or medium.
4. Write each student's name under the appropriate category.
5. When in doubt about particular students, write their names on the chalkboard between the two closest categories. Then select a student, whose classification is rather obvious, from each of the two nearest categories. Ask each child separately to read aloud the poem, followed by the student whose classification is questionable. This approach should be preceded by the remark, "Listen carefully and see if you feel Mary's voice sounds in pitch more like Ruth's voice (high) or more like Jane's voice?" (medium).

The following poem for intermediate grade students illustrates the use of particular voice groupings appropriate for expressing different phrases in the text.

What Will I Do With My Horse? [23]

Med:	Grandfather gave me a horse,
	A clippety, cloppety horse;
High:	A puffy, white kitty
	Can live in the city
Low:	And so can a doggy
	Or Johnny's pet froggy;
All:	But what will I do with a horse?
Med:	What shall I do with my horse,
	My clippety, cloppety horse?
Low:	My horse is so balky
	And so big and gawky;
High:	I've no barn to sleep him
	And no way to keep him;
All:	Oh, what will he do with his horse?
Med:	Guess what I did with my horse?
	My clippety, cloppety horse;
High:	The part that needs feeding
Low:	I gave to my mother,
High:	At night when he's tired,
Low:	He belongs to my brother,
High:	Dad's is the share to be pastured and driven,
Low:	What's left is for me and needs nothing but loving;
Med:	Now Mother and Father and Brother and I
All:	Have a clippety, cloppety . . . Balky and gawky
	But oh, such a very nice horse!

The teacher should first read aloud the poem, with the class listening and following in their books.[24] The children should

[23] From *Verse Choir in the Elementary School* by Clifford E. Barton, Educational Publishing Corp., Darien, Conn., 1954. Used by permission.

[24] Choral speaking may also be done on the kindergarten–first grade level, before children have learned to read. They may simply learn the poem by rote from the teacher.

then identify new words and discuss the meaning and mood of the poem. The teacher should assist the children in relating their ideas of the poem's meaning and mood to previous experiences. The teacher should then point out and demonstrate the rhythmic flow of the words. Finally, the class should practice reading the poem aloud together.

After a new poem has been introduced and the children have a general conception of it, the teacher may wish to further clarify meanings and improve the effectiveness of the choral speaking in general. To this end the teacher might suggest that the children use a vocal tone quality which assists in portraying particular word meanings. Words such as "softly," "thunder," "fluffy," "roaring," and so forth, are a natural beginning point. In conjunction with this the children's attention should be directed toward the different dynamic levels—loud, quiet, or medium—which are called for by particular words and phrases. The children should also be made aware of the different characteristics of high, medium, and low pitches and should endeavor to retain these qualities when reciting the poem. Mood, dynamics, and pitch tend to be blended together in discussion and it is true that in the final recitation they should be completely integrated. In the beginning, however, they are best approached as distinct elements.

Generally the next step is to ask the class to emphasize what they think are the important words and phrases of the poem. The children might clap their hands at each point of stress until they are familiar with this concept. They should also look for phrases which seem to say "please hurry" or "slow down."

Culminating activities are important in any learning sequence. A short program or school assembly arranged around such classroom work will give motivation and direction for future learning experiences in this area.

Following are publications suggested for those who seek further information on choral speaking and poems suitable for various grade levels.

Abney, Louise, and Rowe, Grace. *Choral Speaking Arrangements for the Lower Grades.* Magnolia, Mass.: Expression Company, 1953. (Primary Grades).

Abney, Louise. *Choral Speaking Arrangements for Upper Grades.* Magnolia, Mass.: Expression Company, Revised, 1953. (Intermediate Grades).

Arbuthnot, May Hill. *Time for Poetry.* Chicago: Scott Foresman & Co., 1951. (Primary Grades).

Barton, Clifford E. *Verse Choir in the Elementary School.* Darien, Conn.: Educational Publishing Corp., 1945. (Primary and Intermediate Grades).

Enfield, Gertrude. *Verse Choir Technique.* Magnolia, Mass.: Expression Company, 1937. (Intermediate Grades).

Hemphill, E. Irene. *Choral Speaking and Speech Improvement.* Darien, Conn.: Educational Publishing Corp., 1945. (Primary Grades).

Topics for discussion

1. Why should a creative approach to teaching permeate all avenues of musical experience, *i.e.,* singing, playing, rhythmic activities, and listening to music?

2. In what ways may creative activity contribute to the musical, emotional, and social development of children?

3. What conditions are requisite to creative activity in the classroom and how can they be achieved by the teacher?

4. Why is motivation so important to the successful completion of creative activity?

5. How does the existence, or nonexistence, of creative work in other fields, such as language arts, social studies, and art education, affect the attitudes and accomplishments of children in the music class?

Suggestions for further study

ELLISON, Alfred. *Music with Children*. New York: McGraw-Hill Book Co., Inc., 1959, Ch. 8.

FOX, Lillian M. and HOPKINS, Thomas L. *Creative School Music*. Morristown, N.J.: Silver Burdett Co., 1936, Chs. 4, 5, 6 & 10.

MATHEWS, Paul W. *You Can Teach Music*. New York: E. P. Dutton & Co., Inc., 1958, Ch. 8.

MURSELL, James L. *Music Education: Principles and Programs*. Morristown, N.J.: Silver Burdett Co., 1956, Ch. 12.

NYE, Robert E. and NYE, Vernice T. *Music in the Elementary School*. 2nd Edition. Englewood Cliffs, N.J.: Prentice-Hall, Inc., 1964.

WILT, Miriam E. *Creativity in the Elementary School*. New York: Appleton-Century-Crofts, Inc., 1959.

Films

Melody In Music (Coronet Instructional Films, 65 E. South Water St., Chicago, Ill.), 1952, b&w or color, 13 min., Elem./Col.

Music for Children (Contemporary Films, 267 West 25th St., New York, N.Y. 10001), 1958, b&w, 13 min., Col.
     This film illustrates the Carl Orff method of teaching music to children. Adapted by the National Film Board of Canada.

7 Teaching music reading

Music reading is an integral part of the total music education program, not a skill taught separately and developed in isolation from other music activities. It should be developed as a part of planned experiences in singing, playing, rhythmic activity, listening, and creative expression. Careful consideration of the relationship of music reading to each of these avenues of musical experience can lead to increased musical growth. The development of a reasonable degree of skill in music reading enables children to interpret music notation more readily. As the reading process becomes more efficient, the learning of new music becomes less tedious and more enjoyable. Continuing to learn music through a semi-rote process can have a most stultifying effect upon more mature learners. The development of optimal skills in music reading enables children to ultimately explore the vast wealth of music literature that is an integral part of our culture.

The process of music reading

Music reading is the process of translating the symbols on the printed page into organized, meaningful sound. This process involves, (a) the visual recognition of tonal and rhythmic patterns, (b) the recall or remembrance of how these patterns sound, and (c) the actual production, either singing or playing, of the notated sounds. This process is basically the same whether a person is singing or playing an instrument. The singer has only his "musical memory" upon which to rely. If his experiences with tonal and rhythmic patterns have been meaningful and if the impressions are sufficiently strong, then he will be more likely to produce the desired musical sounds. If his impressions or associations are hazy and unclear he will have difficulty in singing the notation. The instrumentalist is also able to rely upon muscle memory, or kinesthesis.[1] But the instrumentalist must do more than simply depress a combination of keys. To play accurately and in tune the instrumentalist must also possess a clear concept of how the notated patterns should sound before he depresses the keys. It is for this reason that the statement has often been made, "If you can't sing it, you can't play it!" Some instrumental music teachers, therefore, periodically request their students to sing a particularly troublesome tonal pattern for the purpose of clarifying in the player's minds the relationship of the various tones. To summarize, then, music reading involves three aspects: *seeing, thinking,* and *doing, i.e.,* observing the printed page, thinking or recalling what the notation should sound like, and actually producing the sound through singing or playing an instrument.

Music reading readiness

How is the seemingly complicated process of teaching music reading accomplished and when is it begun? Children are usually provided individual song books in the second grade. This is but the beginning of one stage of development. If these initial experiences with notation are to be meaningful the children must be *ready* for the experience. From an awareness of this important necessity has grown the term *readiness*. Readiness

---

[1] For a further discussion of this term, see Norman Munn, *Psychology,* Fourth Edition, Boston: Houghton Mifflin, 1961, pp. 550-551.

implies that the student's physical, social, intellectual, and emotional development is adequate for the undertaking of a particular task.[2] Readiness is used in connection with a student's preparedness to undertake any new task, whether it be in reading, language, new concepts in arithmetic, new activities in physical education, or reading music. Readiness for reading a language depends upon a child's possessing a basic vocabulary of words, the ability to express himself verbally reasonably well, and a curiosity about words and a desire to understand what they mean. Likewise, readiness to undertake the study of the musical score is dependent upon children having had a varied experience with music, including, specifically, the following experiences and capabilities:

1. A repertoire of a considerable number of songs and the ability to sing them reasonably well.
2. A well-established concept of high and low pitch, fast and slow tempi, loud and soft dynamics, and an awareness of mood in songs and in instrumental music.
3. The ability to express simple thoughts creatively through singing.
4. Fundamental experiences with rhythmic activities: walking, running and skipping to music; rapping, tapping and clapping the pulsation of the music; and creative interpretation of music through bodily movement, such as swaying like a tree, marching like a soldier, or dancing like an Indian.
5. Experiences in playing a variety of simple rhythm instruments, hearing other instruments used as an accompaniment to singing, and listening to recordings of instrumental music.
6. Experience in scanning the printed page of music primers, looking at the pictures, discovering familiar and unfamiliar words, and noticing the up and down movement of music notation.

2 Ralph L. Pounds and Robert L. Garretson, *Principles of Modern Education,* New York: Macmillan and Company, 1962, p. 232.

7. A desire to understand the meaning of music notation
   —what it says!

Children should have these experiences during the kindergarten and first grade. They constitute the core of experience
which leads to music reading readiness. Children attempting to
understand the musical score without adequate preparatory background are likely to become frustrated, and as a result some
may develop a dislike for music because of their failure to accomplish teacher-expected tasks. At the very least, without
adequate preparation they will not make a sufficient amount
of progress to justify the introduction of notation in the second
grade. If the above objectives have all been accomplished during
the kindergarten and the first grade, then readiness for undertaking the study of notation in the second grade has been
achieved. Notation of music is simply a visual picture of what
children should have heard through their ears and experienced
through movement of their bodies.

Approaches to the teaching-learning situation

Procedures utilized for teaching music reading must
be *meaningful* and *enjoyable*. Time devoted to abstract drills
totally unrelated to music are generally a waste of time. Whenever
possible, activities should emanate from the music being studied.
But the question may arise, "What about drill? Will it help or
hinder?" The answer to this question depends upon the age,
maturity and goals of the learners. When, for example, the purpose of drill is properly understood by a serious piano student,
it may then be highly appropriate. For a class of children in the
primary grades, however, drill to any great extent generally
defeats its own purpose. For older children a moderate amount of
drill, the purpose of which is understood by the group, may be
of some benefit if presented in an appropriate manner. Some

years ago certain teachers seemed to advocate drill for drill's sake! Perhaps uncertain of their objectives and unaware of the effect their teaching had upon the class, they rather blindly followed a procedure they felt to be correct. Perhaps to some extent they were influenced by the belief that "hard work is good for you"—even for young children.

The attitude of the teacher and the approach he uses in teaching has considerable effect upon children's achievement. Music, being an art, must be a pleasurable activity if students are to benefit from it. The approach utilized in teaching music reading should be designed to arouse curiosity, excite, and impel the group toward participation in the teacher-suggested activity. This objective can often be achieved when the teacher approaches the activity with anticipation, and when the students are led to a recognition of the *need* for comprehending the musical score. In maintaining excitement about the activity, the teacher will find that the maximum degree of learning will occur. Only through pleasurable experiences with music will children ever develop the desire to learn the symbols representing it.

Specific preparatory experiences

Certainly, we all know high school and college students, as well as adults, who still continue to learn their music through a semi-rote process. From their past experiences with music they have gained a rather general understanding of the "ups and downs" of the melodic line. Seated next to a singer with some proficiency, they are often able to learn the music fairly rapidly. If this other singer is, perchance, absent from one rehearsal, they are likely to be in a quandary. Developing individual confidence, security, and the ability to sing without always relying on others may be considered as important and specific goals of music education.

But how does one develop independence? It may result from a long series of well-planned and highly successful experiences involving the study of the musical score. "Well-planned" implies that the experiences are adapted to the needs, interests, and capabilities of the group of learners. "Highly successful" implies that the experiences develop one's musical memory so that tonal relationships and the correct duration of rhythmic patterns may be recalled when reading music. "Highly successful" must also imply that the experiences are of such a nature so as to develop confidence and security within the individual, for lack of these conditions will often prevent children from reading music adequately.

In the second grade, when children are usually first provided with individual songbooks, the basic learning procedure might be best described as a *hearing, doing,* and *seeing* process. Children should hear lots of music; they should learn to sing or play it by imitation; and they should then be led into observing on the printed page what they have sung or played. This procedure is sometimes called the "rote-note process." Through this approach children are gradually led to a clearer and more complete understanding of notation and what it represents—organized rhythm and melody.

The teacher may begin by asking the class to turn to a specific page of their books and examine a song that they have sung but not seen in notation. He might ask, "Do you know this song?" or "Do you recognize this song?" If the answer is "Yes," the question which should follow is "Why?" Most of the group will undoubtedly say that they recognize the title or some of the words. The next question might be, "If this song did not have a title or words, would you still recognize it?" The answer is likely to be "No."

The children may be told that the notation is simply a "picture" of what they have already heard and sung, and that "notes" are placed on a "staff" to tell us how high or low, and how long, each pitch is to be sung. Both the staff and some simple notation should be illustrated on the blackboard at this point. Then the teacher may say, "Boys and girls, as I sing the song, follow the words, and the notes above them, and see if you can tell me what happens." It is hoped the children will notice that when the teacher sings an ascending passage the notes also ascend on the printed page. And as he sings lower, the notes descend on the printed page. This can be an important musical discovery for the class.

The teacher may most profitably "diagram" a song by writing on the chalkboard diagonal lines and arrows to indicate the ascending and descending phrases in the song.

etc.

After this idea has been placed in the children's minds, a few students may be asked to come to the chalkboard and also diagram the song as the class sings. The children should have considerable experience with this activity and *all* individuals should have the opportunity to diagram a variety of songs. On subsequent lessons, the teacher may develop a further degree of discrimination by asking the class which of the following lines and arrows best represents the contour of the musical phrase.

or

Following this activity, the teacher should point out that melodies are built scalewise or stepwise and that some notes are repeated. Through the careful examination of many songs children will develop a clearer understanding of this concept.

Initial experiences in rhythm may simply be the development of an awareness of notes having different durations in the patterns of songs. The teacher should call attention to the fact that some notes move slowly, while others move more quickly. By drawing horizontal lines on the chalkboard representing the approximate durational values of notes these differences may be illustrated. The first phrase of "America" might be illustrated as follows:

To develop a feeling for differences in duration, the children should be allowed ample experience at the chalkboard with this type of activity. At times, it will be desirable for most of the class to sing, while observing a few children at the chalkboard. At other times, it will be best for the children at their seats to illustrate duration on a sheet of paper, while the teacher either sings the song or plays it on the piano.

Children should have many experiences in examining the musical score. They should be asked to look for (a) phrases that are alike, (b) phrases that are different, and (c) phrases that are similar. For example, the teacher may ask the class to look closely at the first phrase. He will then ask them to look for another phrase that is just like the first one and to "frame" it. Framing simply involves using the index fingers of both hands to surround on both sides a particular musical phrase or melodic pattern. Framing has two advantages: it sets apart the particular phrase or melodic pattern so that it bears closer scrutiny; and it enables the teacher, by walking up and down the aisles, to determine rather quickly whether or not the students understand his directions and if they are learning what he wants them to learn. As children mature and develop in their skill of comprehending the printed page, they may be asked to identify many things about the musical score. As previously suggested, they may be asked to examine the first phrase of a song carefully, and then to look for a phrase that is like it; then one that is different; and then one that is similar, but not identical. The teacher may write a pattern on the chalkboard and ask the class to frame the first such pattern in a particular song. He might then ask the class to count the number of such patterns in the song.

In studying music notation, the problem of learning is somewhat compounded by the complexity of the task, which involves pitch and tonality, rhythmic duration, and often reading a text. Therefore, it is often desirable to utilize procedures involving either melody or rhythm singly. The following two sections contain a variety of such approaches.

Approaches through melody

Through the experience of singing numerous songs and listening to many melodies, a child will develop a general awareness of tonality and a realization that music has a tonal center or "home base" around which the other tones revolve, some above and some below. This concept, however vague when first realized, can be clarified through the use of syllables or numbers, and to some extent through letter names. The purpose of using such devices is to help the students find the key center and to understand the relationship between the various notes in the scale or key.

The advantages of syllables are that they are easily singable from the vocal standpoint and that there is a definite syllable assigned to each step in the chromatic scale. The disadvantage of syllables is that they have no meaning whatsoever to children when first introduced. The advantage of numbers is that the terminology is familiar to children and the relationships between these numbers have some meaning. A basis for teaching intervals is thus provided. The disadvantages are that they are not easy to sing and no feasible plan exists for singing the chromatics. Some teachers have their students sing the letter names of the different pitches in a song. The main disadvantage of this procedure is that it is awkward to sing chromatics. (An extra syllable is required for some notes, *i.e.,* F sharp, or B flat.)

Weighing the advantages and disadvantages of each of the above alternatives, some teachers elect to use *one* or *none* of these procedures. Other teachers feel that both syllables and numbers have relatively little value in helping children to clarify tonal relationships, and that the only way to teach music reading is through the use of simple wind instruments, such as the Flutophone, Songflute, Tonette, or the Recorder. Certainly no one can deny the value of these instruments in contributing to children's musical development. But rather than using only one of these accepted systems for teaching tonal relationships, it would seem that in today's modern school there is room for them all. Each has its own particular merits and each may make a unique contribution to a child's musical development. Children are not the same—each child may react somewhat differently to a learning situation; one approach may have more appeal and be more meaningful to a particular child than will another. More important still, however, is that children need to experience tonality in as wide a variety of media as possible—through syllables, numbers, letter names, and various types of instruments. These varied experiences serve to reinforce each other and their combined total effect will prove beneficial to children. A teacher may feel that he will be unable to find adequate time for the pursuance of all the suggested approaches. If so, he should stress one approach, but not to the complete exclusion of the others.

Single tones are unimportant out of the context of the music. The teacher must realize that regardless of the approach used, the students should learn to identify tonal patterns or groups of tones. After all, children do not learn to read language through identifying one letter at a time, but initially by the recognition of single words and later by entire phrases.

The *Tonic Sol-fa* (or movable *Do*) is a system of ear-training in which different syllables are assigned to each degree of the chromatic scale. In learning this system, singers are trained to recognize and, as a result, sing more readily the notated intervals. Eye-ear relationships are thus strengthened through the study and singing of syllables.

Syllables may be best introduced by rote as an additional verse to a familiar song. After the teacher's presentation of the song he may explain that each of the syllables represents a different scale step, and that after the class has become well acquainted with them they will help in singing songs more accurately. Students should sing many familiar songs with syllables (or numbers). This experience will help to establish more firmly various tonal patterns in the children's minds. As a means of providing variety, the teacher might sing the syllables to particular songs and then ask the children to guess each title. After the class has a reasonable familiarity with syllables, the teacher will find it profitable to utilize a variety of other devices and procedures.

Teaching syllabic patterns.   Some of the more frequently occurring melodic patterns in elementary music series are *mi-re-do, sol-la-sol, do-ti-la-sol, sol-do,* and *mi-fa-sol.* The teacher may first sing these various syllable patterns, with the class imitating. After the children have had considerable experience in singing these patterns, he may suggest that they play a game: the teacher sings the patterns on a neutral syllable (after singing *do*) and the class sings back the correct syllables for each tonal pattern. The above patterns are suggested as only a beginning point. The teacher should then select specific patterns from familiar songs in the song books designed for the grade level being taught.

Introducing the diatonic scale.   For another approach the teacher may select a song familiar to the class and point to the appropriate syllables as the children sing them. The scale is displayed on the chalkboard as shown below. This procedure is also an excellent means of introducing the diatonic scale, showing visually the relationship between one scale step and another.

re
—————
do

ti
- - - - - -
la

sol

fa

mi

re

do
—————
ti

la
- - - - - -

Another device to portray the diatonic scale is to illustrate it in the form of a ladder. The rungs of the ladder between the third and fourth degrees and between the seventh degree and the octave should be placed rather closely together to show this half-step relationship. These tonal relationships should be pointed out to the children and they should be asked to listen carefully as they sing the scale with either syllables or numbers.

do	8
ti	7
la	6
sol	5
fa	4
mi	3
re	2
do	1

In addition to listening for the half-steps between *mi* and *fa* (3 and 4), and *ti* and *do* (7 and 8), the class should experience the strong upward pull which both the third and seventh scale degrees have toward their upper neighbors. One way to illustrate this is to ask the class to sing an ascending scale beginning on *do,* then stopping and holding *mi.* They will sense the pull toward *fa.* Also sing the ascending scale and stop on *ti.* They will also sense the upward pull toward *do.* To illustrate the pull toward the tonal center or *do,* have the class sing the ascending scale beginning on *do* upward for an octave, and then sing downward stopping on any particular tone. The feeling of incompleteness will be felt by the group and most will desire to continue the descending scale downward to its natural resting place of *do.*

In addition to using the visual device of a ladder to illustrate the diatonic scale, it is desirable to utilize the piano keyboard, the melody bells (turned on end), and the fingers of the hand to show the up and down movement of the scale. In using the hand for such an illustration, the teacher may point with the index finger of the other hand to the fingers and the spaces between, simulating the lines and spaces of the musical staff.

After introducing the concept of the diatonic scale, the whole and half steps, and *do* or *la* as the tonal center or "home base," the teacher may contrast these major and minor tonalities with songs written using the Pentatonic scale. This five-tone scale uses the first, second, third, fifth, and sixth degrees, but not the fourth and seventh degrees, of the diatonic scale. In songs written in the Pentatonic scale the melody is likely to end anywhere.

Hand signals.   Various positions of the hand, each representing a different scale step, are used in the Kodály method, as well as by other European music educators.[3] *Do,* is a closed

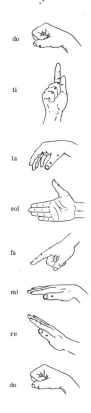

do

ti

la

sol

fa

mi

re

do

---

[3] Some sources accredit the development of hand signals to the English clergyman and publisher John Curwin (1816-1880); other sources indicate their much earlier use.

fist; *re,* an open hand with the palm facing diagonally upward; *mi,* an open hand with the palm facing downward; *fa,* a clenched hand with the thumb and forefinger pointing diagonally downward; *sol,* an open hand with the thumb pointing upward and the palm facing the body; *la,* a relaxed hand with the fingers and thumb pointing downward; and *ti,* a closed hand with the thumb and forefinger pointing upward. Through these hand signals children are helped to *hear* through their ears what they *see* through their eyes. After the children have had some experience with these signals, the teacher may utilize them for ear-training exercises, involving various intervals and melodic patterns. They may also be used to assist children whenever difficulties occur in the singing of songs.[4]

The line-space concept.   In clarifying the purpose of the staff, the teacher should make sure the children understand the line-space concept for scales and chords. That is:

> *line line line*   or   *space space space*   for chords;
> *line space line*   or   *space line space*   for scale passages.

This concept is illustrative of one of a number of understandings which teachers sometimes take for granted, without realizing that children might not comprehend it.

Identifying tonal patterns.   After the students have an understanding of the purposes of the staff, the teacher may select a tonal pattern from a familiar song, write it on the chalkboard, and then, after giving the class the title of the song and the page number, ask them to locate it in the song by framing the pattern with their index fingers. This procedure of comparing a pattern on the chalkboard with those in the books is helpful in training the eye to identify the more minute differences in music notation. While this device facilitates visual development, aural development may occur when the teacher sings a phrase of a song, using a neutral syllable, rather than writing it on the

---

[4] For further information in regard to the use of hand signals, as well as the Kodály method, see Mary Helen Richards, *Threshold To Music,* San Francisco: Fearon Publishers, 1964. See also, Arpad Darazs and Stephen Jay, *Sight and Sound,* Oceanside, N. Y.: Boosey & Hawkes, Inc., 1965.

chalkboard. The students are asked to identify the phrase in the song by relating to the teacher the words beneath the music, or by framing the appropriate phrase. Initially, the students may be able to identify such phrases by observing the general configuration of the notation or the "ups and downs" of the music. As they grow in their capacity to identify phrases, or perhaps motives, they will become increasingly aware of the precise differences in the musical notation.

"Music building" games are another device that will help to cement eye-ear relationships. To prepare for these "games," the students should each draw a staff with about an inch between the lines, and make approximately five noteheads about the size of a quarter from black construction paper. After this basic equipment has been prepared, the group is ready to play a game. The teacher says: *"Do* is on the first space, so place one of your notes there. I will sing *do,* followed by two other notes. See if you can place them on the proper lines or spaces on the staff." Suggested patterns to use in the beginning are *do, re, mi,* and *do, mi, sol.* As the children progress in the development of this skill, the teacher may use a variety of patterns, preferably selected from the song repertoire of the children.

Singing sequential patterns.   The learning and singing of sequential patterns can be a beneficial device for developing greater familiarity with and flexibility in the use of syllables. They should, however, be used in moderation and approached in a "game-like" manner. Extensive drill should be diligently and scrupulously avoided, as such an approach is inappropriate for elementary school children and would only lead to frustration and perhaps dislike of the music activity. The following sequential patterns can be a challenging and enjoyable activity if students will first learn them with accuracy and then endeavor to develop increased speed.

Ascending: *do-mi, re-fa, mi-sol, fa-la, sol-ti, la-do, ti-re, do.*
Descending: *do-la, ti-sol, la-fa, sol-mi, fa-re, mi-do, re-ti, do.*

Ascending: *do-mi-sol, re-fa-la, mi-sol-ti, fa-la-do, sol-ti-re, do.*

Descending: *do-la-fa, ti-sol-mi, la-fa-re, sol-mi-do, fa-re-ti, do.*

Ascending: *do-re-mi, re-mi-fa, mi-fa-sol, fa-sol-la, sol-la-ti, la-ti-do, ti-do-re-do.*

Descending: *do-ti-la, ti-la-sol, la-sol-fa, sol-fa-mi, fa-mi-re, mi-re-do, re-do-ti-do.*

The following sequential pattern is also a good warm-up device for singers and choral groups on any level.

Ascending: *do-re-do,*
do-re-mi-re-do,
do-re-mi-fa-mi-re-do,
do-re-mi-fa-sol-fa-mi-re-do,
do-re-mi-fa-sol-la-sol-fa-mi-re-do,
do-re-mi-fa-sol-la-ti-la-sol-fa-mi-re-do,
do-re-mi-fa-sol-la-ti-do-ti-la-sol-fa-mi-re-do.

Descending: *do-ti-do,*
do-ti-la-ti-do,
do-ti-la-sol-la-ti-do,
do-ti-la-sol-fa-sol-la-ti-do,
do-ti-la-sol-fa-mi-fa-sol-la-ti-do,
do-ti-la-sol-fa-mi-re-mi-fa-sol-la-ti-do,
do-ti-la-sol-fa-mi-re-do-re-mi-fa-sol-la-ti-do.

Teaching letter names.   Knowing the letter names of the staff is a desirable understanding for children to have. In addition to syllables and numbers, it provides them with one further point of intervalic relationship and is also necessary for naming and understanding keys and key relationships. For years teachers have endeavored to teach letter names by associating familiar names and word series with these letter names (*e.g.,* "FACE" and "Every Good Boy Does Fine"). Although there is nothing wrong with using this procedure as a means of introducing the letter names, the fact remains that in spite of all the "crutches" used, including the identification of words from patterns placed on the chalkboard, children have generally not been very successful in remembering this information. One might ask, just what is the difficulty with such learning situations? The answer is reasonably simple. To learn information adequately, students must have a reason for doing so! Students who express themselves musically *only* through singing generally have no real purpose for learning or remembering letter names. Some students will learn this information for a particular test and will then soon forget it if the information is not put into constant use in some way or another.

The only successful means by which one may teach letter names is through the use of simple instruments such as the Tonette, Flutophone, melody bells, and resonator bells. Here there is an ever present need to know the letter names. One needs to know how B, for example, is fingered on a simple instrument, and when to play this pitch. Letter names are essential for instrumental study, whereas the use of syllables or numbers would have relatively little application.

One pitfall which exists in teaching music reading is that the procedures for teaching—singing syllables, numbers, etc.— may become the end objective rather than the means of developing musical memory.[5] Teachers, therefore, should be especially careful to relate all the above-mentioned devices to the specific problem of music reading—for that is the objective toward which they were devised.

Approaches through rhythm

Before examining the printed score and attempting to understand its meaning, children should have had a variety of types of experience with rhythm. They should have had experiences in responding to the pulsation of music through playing rhythm instruments, rapping, tapping, clapping and marking activities, and through walking and marching to music.

[5] See Archie N. Jones, *Music Education in Action*, Boston: Allyn and Bacon, Inc., 1960, p. 113.

They also should have had experiences in duration through playing a "melody rhythm" with rhythm instruments, and through running and skipping to music. They should have learned concepts of fast and slow through creative bodily movement, moving slowly like an elephant and quickly like a fairy, and through various listening lessons on tempo and mood. It is upon this total foundation of rhythmic experience that we endeavor to make duration more meaningful. This is initially accomplished by having the children associate the rhythmic duration of various notes with their past experiences in rhythm. Only thusly can it ever become meaningful.

Real Name	Symbol	Descriptive Names
Quarter note	♩	walking note
Eighth notes	♫	running notes
Quarter and eighth notes	♩ ♪	skipping notes
Eighth note triplets	♪♪♪ (3)	galloping notes
Half note	♩ (half)	a slow note (or step, bend)
Whole note	o	a note to hold

The teacher should, of course, call the student's attention to the difference between the various notes on the printed page. Notes may be referred to by their real names, but to young children this name will not hold much meaning, nor will it be likely to be remembered until after they gain considerable experience with the printed notation. In the initial stages, it is desirable to refer to notes by names descriptive of their length of duration. That is, quarter notes are referred to as "walking notes," and eighth notes as "running notes," and so on. Some teachers prefer to use a double reference, *i.e.*, "This is a quarter note and its play name is 'the *walking* note' because that is the tempo at which it moves."

A former practice followed by some teachers in teaching a song was to have the children first scan the page, looking for walking, running, and skipping notes, etc., and to then, before singing, have them chant the entire song through, using the appropriate "play names." Some basic music textbooks were even designed so as to include songs appropriate for this procedure. Today's modern music series, however, make such a procedure somewhat more difficult, because the songs included are selected on the basis of their musical merits (and rightly so) rather than as a combination of notes that are easy for a group to chant. Nevertheless, chanting still has some merit and, when songs include a combination of notes adaptable to this procedure, it may prove beneficial. It is not necessary to always chant the entire song. This may prove tedious, delay the process of singing, and become unenjoyable and detrimental to the development of positive attitudes toward music. The teacher should select certain basic rhythm patterns in the music and have the class chant them. For example, the children may chant, while clapping the hands, this pattern:

    Quarter   Quarter   Eighth   Eighth   Half

It is also helpful for the teacher to call the children's attention to the difference in color between the black notes (♩) and the white notes (♩). By dramatizing this point somewhat, a more vivid impression is made on the child of the specific differences between quarter and half notes.

In approaching the study of rhythm, the teacher should use a variety of procedures, some which emphasize an aural approach and others which stress the visual aspects.

Rhythmic conversation.   The teacher may utilize a "rhythm conversation" with children (or "rhythm talk," as some persons prefer to call it), *i.e.,* the teacher raps, taps, or claps, or sings on a neutral syllable a rhythmic pattern, and the children then imitate it.[6] For example:

This aural experience will contribute toward the development of more careful listening habits. It is suggested that the rhythm patterns utilized for "rhythm talk" be selected from song books appropriate to the grade level being taught.

Teaching concepts of duration.   In examining the musical score, the teacher may help children to identify the note that moves with the beat (♩), the notes that move faster than the beat (♫), and the notes that move slower than the beat (♩). These notes may be referred to by their actual names and the class may clap and/or chant the rhythm of the song.[7] This concept may be introduced as early as the second grade, depending, of course, upon the background and capabilities of the children. As children gain experience these relationships will be broadened and clarified. The concepts may be reinforced by clapping and/or using the three rhythmic patterns as an accompaniment to a song. For example:

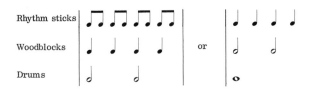

The teacher should stress the fact that we are always dealing in proportions. While two eighth notes always equal a quarter note, the speed of either note is determined by the *tempo* of the music.

[6] In the Carl Orff approach, this basic idea is called Echo Clapping. For further activities growing out of this idea, see Chapter 6, p. 150.

[7] Bjornar Bergethon and Eunice Boardman, *Musical Growth in the Elementary School*, New York: Holt, Rinehart and Winston, Inc., 1963, p. 69.

Developing rhythmic response.   In the study of particular rhythmic patterns, clapping can be most helpful if the teacher helps the children to strive for accuracy. It is most important that children sense the pulse whenever responding to rhythmic patterns of any type. This response may be facilitated if they are asked to squeeze the hands together on every pulsation except those that are clapped. The following example illustrates this approach.

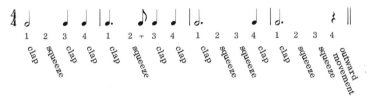

When squeezing, it is natural for the hands to move downward slightly in response to the pulse. This movement should be encouraged. It is also important that children respond to the rests in the music. This may be done appropriately by separating the hands in a slight outward movement.

The teacher may later wish to place rhythmic patterns on the chalkboard, asking the children if they can guess the title of the song before clapping the notated rhythm. This approach places the emphasis upon the visual aspects of notation. At other times the teacher may want to use an aural approach to guessing song titles by rapping, tapping, or clapping rhythmic patterns.

Notating names and words.   Another device that evokes a great deal of interest is to write each child's name in the rhythmic notation prescribed by the duration of each particular syllable. The notation should be written on the chalkboard for the entire class to see. The children may also want to write this notation above their names in their notebooks. Activities such as this have unique value in that it gives children a more personal brand of experience with rhythm.

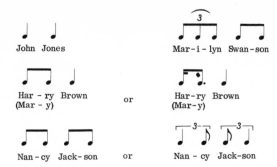

It will be noted that the names of Harry (or Mary) Brown and Nancy Jackson are illustrated in two ways. Depending upon the musical development of the children and their ability to perceive these more subtle differences, it would generally be better to illustrate the names in the latter way, which is certainly more accurate. For younger children, with less experience in notation, the simpler of the two ways should be used. This judgment can be made only by the teacher after he knows and understands his particular groups' capabilities.

From the experience of notating one's own name may grow the desire to learn how other words would look in notation. Following are some words, combinations of which have been used in the past to clarify in student's minds various rhythmic patterns.

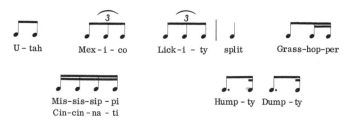

From these and similar experiences children may develop a clearer understanding of the fact that the words of a song determine, to a certain extent, the duration of the notes. Fol-

Clapping the rhythmic patterns of children's names is one way of teaching note values.

lowing these activities, children may wish to notate the rhythm of short sentences or poems. This may lead somewhat naturally into the creating of a song as a class or group endeavor. (See Chapter 6, pp. 143-46 for suggested procedures.)

Teaching concepts of meter, intervals, and tonality

An understanding of the concepts of meter, intervals, and tonality is essential to continued musical growth. Such understanding cannot come about, however, until children have achieved a certain maturity and have had reasonably varied experiences with music. But children will be limited in their further musical development until these concepts are understood. Thus, their study may be considered an important crossroads in the path of musical development.

Meter

A concept of meter is dependent upon experience which first develops a feeling for pulsation in music and an awareness of stress, or accent. In listening to the pulsation of music, children will discover that all the beats do not sound the same. When asked how they differ, a child will usually answer that some beats sound heavier than others. The teacher should at this point provide the children with words which more accurately describe this sound—stress or accent. The teacher should tell the class that most music swings in twos, three, or fours. Ample listening experiences should be provided to clarify this concept. After the class had identified the way in which a particular musical selection swings, a few children should be asked to "mark out" the pulsation and the accents on the chalkboard.

For example: $\frac{2}{4}$ | | | | | | | | | | or $\frac{3}{4}$ ⟳ ° ° ⟳ ° ° ⟳

(See also Chapter 3, p. 56 for other marking patterns.) Activities such as these help to develop the concept of accent through muscular response, as well as through a visual portrayal of the strong and weak beats. Children are, therefore, better able to understand the function of the measure bars which set off these groups of strong and weak beats. (The strong beat in the measure immediately follows the bar line.)

After understanding these concepts, children may be told that the meter signature simply tells them how the music swings, *i.e.,* in twos, threes, or fours, the top number indicating the number of beats in a measure and the bottom number the kind of note that receives one beat. Children should then examine a variety of songs to discover how the music swings. It would then be helpful for the teacher to play part or all of these songs on the piano, with the children clapping the pulse and stressing the accent.

The concept of music swinging in twos, threes, or fours may be introduced relatively early—in the third grade or the latter part of the second grade. However, comprehension of the concept of the bottom number in the meter signature, representing the type of beat note, is dependent upon the group's understanding of the actual names of the notes, their symbols, and the mathematical relationship between them. Often this relationship, based upon fractions, does not become clear until the fourth grade

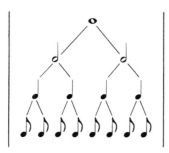

In teaching by analogy, the whole note may be compared to a dollar, the half note to the half dollar, and the quarter note to a quarter, and so on. Concepts of meter and duration may be further strengthened by other visual and aural devices.

The duration of half notes or quarter notes is a relative matter depending upon the designation of the beat note. This concept may be clarified somewhat through the following approach.

Tell the class that the meter is 4/4 and that a quarter note receives one beat, a half note two beats, and a whole note four beats. Then ask the class to tap the basic pulsation (indicated by the teacher). Then play a series of chords, each of the same duration, on the piano and ask the class to count the number of beats in the chords played. Then ask them what kind of note they felt it was. On subsequent lessons the teacher may simply identify the meter, determine or set the pulsation, and play the chord progression. About the time students become accustomed to the quarter note as the beat note, then they may encounter a new meter signature. The teacher may simply announce that 4/2, or 6/8 is the meter signature, describe the number of beats each note receives, and play the durational pattern on the piano.

Following these activities place notation on the chalkboard without bar lines. Then ask the class to determine the meter and place bar lines in the appropriate locations. Initially, select notation from songs familiar to the class so that the device will be as meaningful as possible. For example, the following notation may be placed on the chalkboard:

Bar lines properly placed will result in the following more easily identifiable rhythm:

As children mature in their ability to determine the proper location of bar lines, the teacher may select durational patterns from songs less familiar to the group.

Intervals

An *interval* is a measurement of distance between two pitches. A basic understanding of intervals is helpful in comprehending the musical score. Knowledge of intervals facilitates the placement of the sharps and flats in the key signature and contributes to singer's ability to read music—when he knows, for example, what a third or sixth sounds like and can readily identify them on the printed page.[8]

[8] The intervals in the example below are all major intervals, except the fourth, fifth, and octave, which are perfect intervals. Major intervals, when made one-half step smaller, either by lowering the top pitch or by raising the bottom pitch, become minor intervals. Perfect intervals, when made smaller by one-half step, become diminished intervals. If minor intervals are made smaller by one-half step, they also become diminished intervals. Major and perfect intervals, if made larger by one-half step, either by raising the top pitch or by lowering the bottom, become augmented intervals.

For further information on intervals, see any of the books on music fundamentals listed in the Appendix, pp. 245-47.

Second	Third	Fourth	Fifth	Sixth	Seventh	Octave

The student must be able to recognize intervals both visually and aurally. To determine an interval on the printed page, children should be advised to begin with the bottom note, consider it as the first, and count each line and space up to and including the last, or top note. The total number of lines and spaces counted determine the interval. Children should have some experience in determining intervals based on various pitch levels; they should examine lots of music and determine the intervals between notes at points designated by the teacher.

But if visual recognition of intervals is to be of help at all, children must also know how these intervals sound. The best procedure is to relate the intervals to a meaningful sound that is a part of the children's musical experience. That is, when discussing an interval of a major third, use the reference point of *do-mi, fa-la,* or *sol-ti,* whichever is applicable.

Another approach is to identify the intervals (both ascending and descending) in certain songs that are easily remembered, and which serve as a familiar point of reference. Following are some suggested examples. Children might add to this list familiar songs that they particularly enjoy.

Half steps (semi-tones)
    Ascending—"Stardust"
    Descending—"Habanera" (from *Carmen*), "Ciribiribin"
Major seconds (whole tones)
    Ascending—"America," "Happy Birthday"
    Descending—"I Dream of Jeannie," "Sweet Rosie O'Grady"
Minor thirds
    Ascending—"The More We Get Together"
    Descending—"This Old Man," "Caisson Song," "Everytime I Feel the Spirit"
Major thirds
    Ascending—"On Top of Old Smoky," "I Heard the Bells on Christmas Day"

Descending—"Swing Low, Sweet Chariot"

Perfect fourths

Ascending—"The Farmer in the Dell," "Auld Lang Syne," "Flow Gently Sweet Afton," "Taps"

Descending—"March of the Three Kings" (Bizet), "Praise to God" (*This Is Music*, Bk. 4)

Perfect fifths

Ascending—"Twinkle, Twinkle Little Star," "My Favorite Things" (from *Sound of Music*)

Descending—"My Home's In Montana"

Minor sixths

Ascending—"Go Down, Moses," "Fiddlers Two" (*This Is Music*, Bk. 4)

Major sixths

Ascending—"My Bonnie Lies Over the Ocean," "My Wild Irish Rose," "It Came Upon the Midnight Clear"

Descending—"Nobody Knows the Trouble I've Seen," "Sing Your Way Home" (*Growing With Music*, Bk. 4)

Major sevenths

Ascending—"Calliope" (*Singing In Harmony*, Bk. 6)

Minor sevenths

Ascending—"Bali Hai" [9]

Perfect octaves

Ascending—"Somewhere Over the Rainbow," "The Christmas Song" (by Mel Torme), "Annie Laurie"

The following songs are also helpful in serving as points of reference for major triads.

Ascending—"The Marine's Hymn," "Kum Bah, Yah," "Sarasponda"

Descending—"Star Spangled Banner," "Dixie," "Come Thou Almighty King"

---

[9] While the first two pitches in this song are the interval of an octave, the second pitch, because of its relatively short duration, gives way to the third, thus creating the feeling for the major 7th interval.

Tonality

In turn, if a system of syllables or numbers is to be of any benefit to children, they must know how to find the key-note (*do* or *la*) without depending upon the teacher. Initially, the simplest explanation is to tell the class that, for the sharp keys, the last sharp to the right is *ti*, and to find *do* one simply counts up one step; for flat keys, the last flat to the right is *fa* and to find *do*, simply count down (*fa, mi, re, do*) four scale steps on alternate lines and spaces.

After locating *do*, the students will want to determine if the song is in major or minor tonality. This may be done by scanning the melodic line. Specifically, they should first look to see if the melody begins or ends on *do*. Songs beginning on incomplete measures may start on any one of several pitches, but those in major tonality will generally end on *do*. If the song does not end on *do*, the student should determine if it ends on *la*. If it does, the song is probably in minor tonality. If the song ends on neither *do* nor *la*, then perhaps it is written in the pentatonic scale, which includes the first, second, third, fifth, and sixth degrees—but not the fourth or seventh—of the diatonic scale. Songs based upon the pentatonic scale may end on any scale tone.

Introducing the concept of minor tonality will serve little purpose until children have had considerable experience in singing songs and hearing recorded music in the minor mode, and feel a need to determine the tonality of such music. They are not likely, however, to feel a need until the teacher asks them to find the key note by using the procedures previously described.

By placing a major scale on the chalkboard, with its relative minor key written a third below, children may visually see a relationship. They may then sing both scales, the major scale beginning and ending on *do*, and the minor scale on *la*.

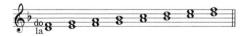

This minor scale written above is called the natural minor scale. Children should be told that the form of the minor scale they are most likely to encounter is the harmonic form, with the raised seventh degree of the scale.

In the melodic form of the minor scale the sixth and seventh degrees of the scale are raised one-half step when ascending and lowered when descending. It will serve little purpose, however, to present information to the children about the melodic form of the minor scale unless the music they are studying is written in the mode and unless they show curiosity about the tonality.

Children should understand how major scales are constructed. Before an explanation is attempted, however, they should have had experience in singing scales and have developed an awareness of the half-steps between the third and fourth and the seventh and eighth degrees of the scale. The experience of observing, while singing, the scale as a ladder with the third and fourth and seventh and eighth rungs close together is also helpful.

With these experiences as a basis, the teacher may show how the diatonic scale is built upon two tetrachords, one superimposed upon the other (the tetrachord is a part of the ancient Greek scale, consisting of four tones in the order of "whole step, whole step, half step.") Children may more readily understand the combination of tones by observing these steps on the piano keyboard. The whole steps are easily noticed because of the placement of the black keys; each black key represents a pitch a half-step higher or lower than the adjacent white key.

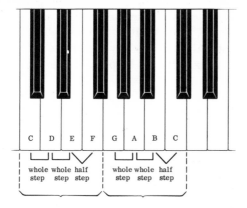

Children should understand that composers cannot always be restricted to the key of C and that they generally begin their "scales" on other pitches. The teacher may then play a scale beginning on G, playing only the white keys. Let as many children as possible observe the piano keyboard while others follow a dummy keyboard or a facsimile of some type. Before the teacher plays the scale he should ask the class to listen carefully to it. The children may wince a bit as the F natural is played. The teacher should then ask them how the scale sounded. Perhaps some children will immediately comprehend why the scale sounded strange. If not, play it again, slowly, asking the class to watch for the "whole, whole, half-step combination." It will eventually become evident that the teacher is playing whole, whole, half step, and whole, half, whole step. The teacher should then ask the class how the latter tetrachord might be corrected. The answer is simply to raise the next to last tone by one half step. This results in the combination of whole, whole, half step. The children should then be told that the way to raise the next to last note in this scale is to place a sharp in front of it. (Using the same procedure for a scale beginning on F, it will become evident to the children that to achieve the right combination of whole and half steps it will be necessary to lower, by using a flat sign, the fourth scale degree.)

Although this procedure may seem somewhat detailed, it is the only way to develop an understanding of the reason for key signatures. To further strengthen this concept the procedure should be illustrated with several other scales, at least those beginning on D, F, and B♭. It is also desirable to devote some time to showing children how key signatures are placed on the staff. The following rules are helpful.

For sharp keys:
  a. The first sharp is on F.
  b. To place the other sharps count down four lines and spaces. (The third and sixth sharps should be placed up an octave).
For flat keys:
  a. The first flat is on B.
  b. To place the other flats count up four lines and spaces. (The third, fifth, and seventh flats are placed down an octave.)
In counting either up or down, make sure the students count the beginning pitch as one and the last pitch as four.

Procedures for solving some specific rhythmic problems

Students' concepts of some rhythmic patterns are likely to be rather vague—they may have a general understanding of the pattern, but are unable to sing or play it with any degree of accuracy. At the appropriate time in the children's musical development, it will be found desirable to isolate these problems from the context of the musical composition and utilize procedures to clarify understanding and improve performance. Any attempt at clarification will be of little value, however, unless the students are aware of the problem and feel a need for improvement. Following are several concepts of rhythm which may be clarified by breaking the problem down into its simplest components and explaining it in a step-wise manner.

Teaching the divided beat.

1. The teacher might write the following pattern on the chalkboard and sing it on a neutral syllable:

2. Next, the teacher should sing the following pattern, changing the second quarter note in the second measure to two eighth notes:

The teacher should then ask the class what the change was, or, if they have difficulty describing the change, ask them how the rhythmic pattern sounded different. The class may simply reply that there were extra notes in the second measure. The teacher should then erase the notes in this measure and write the correct notation (as illustrated above). If certain class members comprehend the precise notation needed, then let one of them come to the chalkboard and write it.

Teaching the dotted note.

1. The teacher and the class should sing the following pattern as he points to the notes:

2. The teacher then alters the notation by indicating a tie between the first and second notes in the second measure:

When singing the above pattern, the second beat in the second measure should be emphasized slightly. This is sometimes known as the "push" note. (Success in teaching the dotted note is dependent upon how well the divided beat is understood.)

3. The teacher should then write a dotted quarter and eighth note on the chalkboard beneath the previous pattern, pointing out that the dot simply takes the place of the first of the two eighth notes. The pattern should appear immediately beneath the other so that students can see the similarity.

This should lead to a further discussion of dotted notes and the introduction of the concept that dotted notes receive half again their normal durational value.

Teaching the after-beat.   Before attempting to analyze the after-beat pattern, it is desirable for the class to have had experience singing some songs or playing music in which this problem is involved. The children, if they learn the music correctly by rote, will have a reasonably correct mental conception of how it sounds. This is essential before the concept can be successfully analyzed. Another way to develop a correct conception is to listen to various recordings which include this rhythmic pattern.

Prior to using the following procedure the teacher should first fully establish the feeling for the pulsation of the music through clapping the hands, tapping the foot, beating the pulsation on the knee, or by conducting.

1. The teacher and the class should sing through the following pattern on a neutral syllable:

2. They should sing the pattern again, accenting the first and third eighth notes in the second measure:

3. They should then sing the pattern without an accent.

4. The class and the teacher should sing the pattern again, accenting the second and fourth eighth notes in the second measure:

5. Finally the class should omit the first and third eighth notes, leaving only the second and fourth eighth notes (*this* is the "after-beat"). To sing the after-beats correctly, the pulsation on the first and third notes in the second measure must be felt:

Developing skill in reading a variety of rhythmic patterns. It is generally helpful if the teacher will place on the chalkboard a variety of rhythmic problems encountered in the songbooks utilized on a particular grade level. The teacher should first establish the tempo and the students should maintain it by tapping their feet, clapping, conducting, or beating the pulsation of the music on their knees. Then, as the teacher points to various measures, the children are to sing the patterns on a neutral syllable. For example:

Procedures for stimulating interest in music reading

One of the best ways to stimulate interest in music reading is to simply *be* an interesting teacher and approach topics with an air of expectancy and enthusiasm, utilizing a variety of types of activities and encouraging and complimenting students on their progress. These are basic conditions for the teacher who endeavors to help students develop toward their maximum capabilities; he should be creative and always alert to ways and means of stimulating children's interest. Following are some procedures that are recommended and which, it is hoped, will call to mind other ideas that the teacher might use.

Writing and studying themes.   Themes from music selected for listening lessons may be notated on the chalkboard in a special location, perhaps with the heading "Themes from our Listening Music." Children may take pride in maintaining their "listening" corners, especially if they are given the opportunity of helping the teacher write part or all of the notation on the chalkboard. The children should analyze and sing these themes on a neutral syllable before listening to them. In addition to the aural experience of singing the themes, actually seeing the themes during the listening period will help the class to remember them.

"Mystery tunes."   Another device which may evoke considerable interest is for the teacher to write on the chalkboard a melody reasonably familiar to the class. Above it he may write the words, "Mystery Tune—Who can identify it?" This theme should be notated before the class enters the room and covered by a map, chart, or movie screen. At the appropriate time during the lesson, the teacher may uncover the music and ask the class if they can identify it. If the children's natural curiosity is aroused and if the teacher's approach presents a challenge to the class, then they will be likely to draw upon all their musical knowledge in an effort to identify the tune. Often the question may be asked, "Will you tell us how to find out the tune?" Of

course, this is the question that teachers hope for, because they know that learning is not likely to occur until the class feels the need for it.

The writer recalls one teacher who taught in a school located in a relatively low socio-economic area and in which the children exhibited only a limited amount of interest in music. This teacher announced in his classes a contest in which all the sixth grades would participate. Toward the end of each period, he planned to reveal the day's new "mystery tune." The class was to study it quietly and discuss its probable title during the homeroom period. Later in the day, the representative of each class would leave with the music teacher the "guess" of his homeroom. This teacher announced that an award would be given at the end of the six-week period to the homeroom with the highest number of correct answers. Needless to say, it was no time at all until the students were clamoring for information as to how to determine the correct tune.[10]

"What's wrong with this melody?"   Still another device for stimulating interest in music reading is for the teacher to write a familiar tune on the chalkboard, and, in the process, deliberately alter several intervals, the rhythmic duration of particular notes, or both. The teacher then asks the class if they can tell what is wrong with the music notation. If students have difficulty in identifying the incorrect notation, have them sing the music, preferably on a neutral syllable so that attention will be focused upon the music rather than on the text. As the students sing, the teacher may point to each note. The wrong notes soon become apparent.

What's Wrong With This Melody?

10 Cf. Frances M. Andrews and Joseph A. Leeder, *Guiding Junior High School Pupils in Music Experiences,* Englewood Cliffs, N.J.: Prentice-Hall, Inc., 1953, pp. 51-53.

Alternative procedures for teaching songs

Teachers need not always use the same standardized procedure for teaching songs. One approach may involve a careful analysis of the music for the purpose of developing tonal and rhythmic independency. This process emphasizes helping the child to interpret for himself the symbols on the printed page. The teacher's role is to guide the students' analysis—not to provide it for him (once a child has heard a song, he no longer has reason to analyze the score in the same way). Reading skills may be developed only through lots of experience in actual reading, *i.e.*, experience in relying upon one's own musical memory in attempting to recall the actual sound of the notation. A suggested teaching procedure, then, for developing skills in music reading is as follows.

1. Have the children *scan* the score looking for familiar and unfamiliar tonal and rhythmic patterns. The teacher may guide the class in, for example, finding phrases that are alike, phrases that are different, phrases that are almost alike but slightly different, finding and framing like tonal and/or rhythmic patterns, and identifying new elements in the score such as unfamiliar tonal and rhythmic patterns, accidentals, or new words.
2. Examine the meter signature. Does the music swing in twos, threes, or fours? (This step may be omitted for very young children until they have reached sufficient maturity to be introduced to the concept.)
3. Chant and/or clap the rhythm of the song. In chanting, the class may respond according to the actual names of the notes. For example: "quarter, quarter, eighth, eighth, half note, etc." In clapping, make sure that the class responds to the pulse by squeezing the hands to-

gether on each pulsation except those that are clapped (see p. 183 for example). It is not always necessary to chant or clap the entire song, but usually only the basic patterns. Call attention to identical rhythmic patterns in various phrases.

4. Examine the key signature and locate *do*. Then determine if the tonal center of the song is *do* or *la*. If it seems to be neither, is it in the Pentatonic mode? (This step may also be omitted for very young children until they have reached sufficient maturity to be introduced to the concept—generally in the fourth grade.)

5. Sing syllables (or numbers) of certain basic tonal patterns.

6. Sing the song.

7. Repeat any of the above steps whenever further clarification of certain aspects of the song is needed.

The above procedure is based upon the idea that children develop skill in reading through experience in analyzing the score and attempting to recall from their musical memory the way the music should sound. A considerable amount of time, therefore, should be devoted to this procedure. Admittedly, however, teaching all songs in this manner is not necessary or even desirable. The procedure is time-consuming, and a teacher may often teach a song with another objective in mind. For example, the teacher may wish to emphasize only the relationship of a particular folk song to the culture from which it emanated. Therefore, he would want the class to learn the song as readily as possible so that the time may be devoted to other aspects of the unit. This procedure will quite naturally involve either the teacher singing the song or playing a recording of it. In this case, once the children have heard the song, it would be of little value as a reading song. The following procedure is then suggested.

1. Provide the children with an overall concept of the song by singing it entirely through, playing a recording of it, or playing it on the piano while the class follows the song in their books.

2. Have the children identify unfamiliar words and then briefly discuss the meaning and mood of the text.

3. Identify the meter and tonality. Does the song swing in twos, threes, or fours? Is the song in major or minor tonality?

4. The class should then sing the song with the teacher.

5. Identify tonal and rhythmic difficulties and endeavor to overcome them. Difficult tonal patterns may be sung slowly with syllables or numbers, and rhythmic problems may be approached through chanting or clapping. Most rhythmic problems, however, may be corrected rather quickly by having the class recite the text in the correct musical rhythm. Once the rhythm is corrected the melodic aspects of the song are sung more readily.

6. Sing the song a second time.

7. Discuss the mood and meaning of the song again, emphasizing what it means to the class and what it may have meant to the folk from whom it emanated.

Topics for discussion

1. Why is it important that students develop at least a minimal degree of skill in reading music?

2. Describe the process of music reading and compare it to the reading of literature.

3. What is *readiness* and why is it important to the undertaking of a particular task? Describe the attitudes, skills and understandings that constitute readiness for music reading.

4. Why is an understanding of the concepts of meter, intervals, and tonality essential to continued musical growth?

5. Discuss the necessity and desirability of using alternative procedures for the teaching of songs in the intermediate grades.

Suggestions for further study

DARAZS, Arpod, and JAY, Stephen. *Sight and Sound: Visual Aid in Melody and Harmony.* Oceanside, N.Y.: Boosey & Hawkes, Inc., 1965.

ELLIOTT, Raymond. *Teaching Music: Methods and Materials for the Elementary Grades.* Columbus, Ohio: Charles E. Merrill Books, Inc., 1960, Ch. 8.

LEONHARD, Charles. *A Song Approach to Music Reading.* Morristown, N.J.: Silver Burdett Company, 1953.

McMILLAN, L. Eileen. *Guiding Children's Growth Through Music.* Boston: Ginn and Company, 1959, Ch. 6.

MYERS, Louise Kifer. *Teaching Children Music in the Elementary School.* Third Edition. Englewood Cliffs, N.J.: Prentice-Hall, Inc., 1961, Ch. 7.

NYE, Robert E., and NYE, Vernice T. *Music in the Elementary School,* 2nd ed. Englewood Cliffs, N.J.: Prentice-Hall, Inc., 1964, Ch. 10.

PIERCE, Ann E. *Teaching Music in the Elementary School.* New York: Henry Holt and Company, 1959, Ch. 7.

PITTS, Lilla Belle, and OTHERS. *Guide and Teaching Suggestions for Our Singing World.* (Grades Four, Five and Six). Boston: Ginn and Company, 1952, pp. 36-79.

RICHARDS, Mary Helen. "The Legacy from Kodály." *Music Educators Journal,* Volume 49, No. 6, June-July, 1963, pp. 27-30.

RICHARDS, Mary Helen. *Threshold to Music.* San Francisco: Fearon Publishers, 1964.

WILSON, Harry R. *Sing a Song at Sight.* Chicago: Schmitt, Hall & McCreary Company, 1954.

Films

Beginning Music Reading (Bailey Films, 6509 De Longpre Ave., Hollywood, Calif. 90028), 1955, b&w or color, 13 min., Col.

Music Reading (Johnson Hunt Productions, 6509 De Longpre Ave., Hollywood, Calif.), 1952, b&w, 20 min., Elem./Col.

Reading Music Series (Coronet Instructional Films, 65 E. South Water St., Chicago, Ill.), 1960. Three films, b&w, 11 min. each. Elem./Col. (1) Learning About Notes, (2) Finding the Rhythm, (3) Finding the Melody.

8 Teaching part-singing

Singing in parts can be a satisfying and enriching experience for children in the intermediate grades. Two-part singing is generally introduced in the fifth grade and three-part singing in the sixth grade. The outmoded procedure of always learning each part separately by rote and then singing them together is, however, decidedly *not* the way to develop skill in part-singing. Students *are* capable of interpreting the printed symbols that represent these parts, but prior to learning to do so they must have had a variety of preparatory aural experiences with harmony. The study of harmonic notation will be relatively meaningless until the sound has been experienced. After students have had a number of successful and meaningful aural experiences with harmony, they may then be led to the process of recognizing and singing those aspects of harmonic notation that they have already experienced by ear.

Preparatory experiences

Readiness to undertake a particular task is essential if children are to be ultimately successful. To provide this necessary background a variety of approaches are needed. Among these it is important to include dialogue songs, chants, descants, rounds and canons, combined songs, harmonized song endings, singing

205

chord roots, harmonizing "by ear," and singing chordal accompaniments. Many of these activities may be introduced in the fourth grade and some even in the latter part of the third grade, depending upon the maturity and background of a particular class. These activities, however, should not be considered as terminal in nature, but may be continued for as long as they contribute to enjoyment and to the musical development of children.

Dialogue songs

In singing a dialogue song the children are generally divided into two groups, one group answering the questions or reiterating the statements made by the other. Thus a conversation or dialogue takes place. In dialogue songs, harmony does not occur except where one part might briefly overlap the other. The value of such songs is that they help to develop tonal awareness and vocal independency. Each student must listen carefully to the singers in his own group, as well as to those in the other, if precision of entrances and releases is to occur. The "teamwork" involved in the effective singing of dialogue songs is one of the basic factors that contributes to their enjoyment.

The spiritual, "Who Did?", shown here, is a particularly good example of a dialogue song. Teachers will find many other songs of this type in the basic song books for the intermediate grades. (See the classified indexes of these books for title listings.)

Chants

The use of chants, based upon simple tonal patterns, may enhance the singing of particular songs and serves as an excellent preparation for later experiences in part-singing. Easy chants may be utilized with children beginning in the latter part of the third grade, depending of course upon their aptitude and previous musical experience. Very easy chants, involving only a few pitches, are particularly adaptable for use with children with a limited vocal range. In singing chants the class should be divided into two equal groups, with each group al-

Who Did? [1]

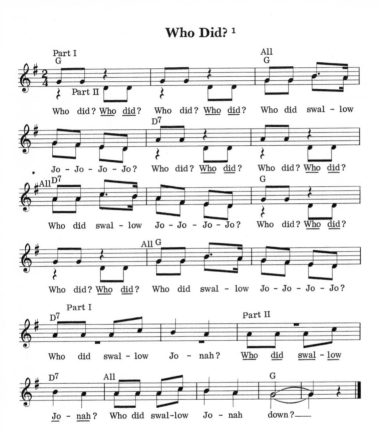

2. Whale did, <u>Whale did</u>, Whale did, <u>Whale did</u>,
   Whale did swallow Jo-Jo-Jo-Jo.
   Whale did, <u>Whale did</u>, Whale did, <u>Whale did</u>,
   Whale did swallow Jo-Jo-Jo-Jo.
   Whale did, <u>Whale did</u>, Whale did, <u>Whale did</u>,
   Whale did swallow Jo-Jo-Jo-Jo.
   Whale did swallow Jonah,
   <u>Whale did swallow Jonah</u>,
   Whale did swallow Jonah up.

[1] From *Music Near and Far, Book Four,* Morristown, N.J.: Silver Burdett Company, 1956, pp. 102-103. Used by permission.

ternately having the opportunity to sing the chant or second part.

While a variety of chants may be located in various books, the teacher may wish to devise his own. Songs with a minimum of harmonic changes are the most adaptable for such purposes. Rounds that necessitate the use of only one chord are most appropriate for the initial experiences. An extremely simple, but effective chant may be devised by having half the class sing a pattern on the first degree of the scale (*do*), while the other half sings the melody of the song. It is often desirable to use this pattern as a brief "introduction" so that the pitch may be more firmly established in the children's minds. For example, the following tonal and rhythm pattern may be used as a chant with the familiar round, "Row, Row, Row Your Boat."

Row, Row, Row Your Boat

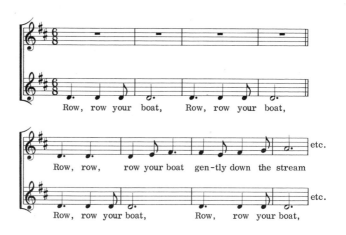

As an alternative approach, the fifth degree of the scale (*sol*) may also be used as a basis for a chant of this round. In addition to using the first and fifth degrees of the scale separately for a chant, the two pitches may be effectively combined for use with some songs. Some examples are as follows:

Three Blind Mice

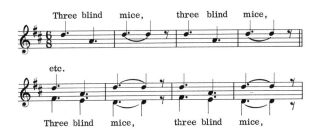

Are You Sleeping

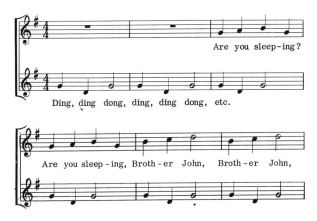

The descending eighth note pattern on the pitches *do, ti, la, sol* provides a simple, but interesting part for such songs as "MacDonald's Farm" and "Lightly Row," as well as many others.

Macdonald's Farm

In the process of devising a chant for a particular song the teacher will want to consider the selection of appropriate words for the melodic and rhythmic pattern. Generally the use of some key word in the text may be adapted for this purpose. As indicated in the round "Are You Sleeping," the words "ding, ding, dong" are appropriate to the melodic pattern of *do, sol, do,* and may be said to simulate ringing bells. Likewise, in the song "MacDonald's Farm," the syllables "Ee-i-o—," also taken from the text, are easily adaptable to the descending eighth note pattern.

The above suggestions are made for the teacher who wishes to devise simple chants for children's initial experiences with harmony. Certainly many other tonal combinations—some much more intricate—are possible and should be utilized. Teachers will find it highly profitable to write some chants for certain favorite songs that are appropriate to each group's background and maturity.

Descants

A descant is a contrasting melody that is sung simultaneously with a familiar song. The descant is generally, but not always, somewhat higher in pitch than the melody and is usually sung by a few selected voices. Melody bells, or a simple wind instrument may also be utilized effectively on the descant part—with or without the added voices. Descants may enhance the effectiveness of many songs commonly used throughout the intermediate grades. They are particularly helpful as a preparation for experiences in part-singing. Simple descants may be introduced in the fourth grade and in some instances the latter part of the third grade, depending, of course, upon the children's aptitude and previous musical experience.

The Mockingbird Song [2]

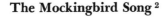

3. If that billy goat won't pull,
   Mammy's goin' to buy you a cart and bull.
   If that cart and bull turn over,
   Mammy's goin' to buy you a dog named Rover.

*Upper part may be sung, or played by a melody instrument.

2 From *Music Across Our Country,* Chicago: Follett Publishing Company, 1958, p. 140. Used by permission.

All Through the Night [3]

Loo_____ Loo loo loo loo

1. Sleep, my child, and   peace at-tend thee   all   thro' the night,
2. While   the moon her   watch is keep-ing   all   thro' the night,

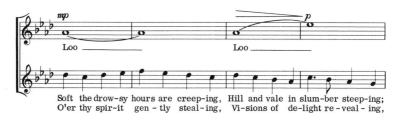

Loo_____ Loo loo loo loo

Guard - ian an - gels God will send thee   all   thro' the night;
While   the wea - ry   world is sleep-ing   all   thro' the night,

Loo _____   Loo _____

Soft the drow-sy hours are creep-ing, Hill and vale in slum-ber steep-ing;
O'er thy spir-it gen-tly steal-ing, Vi-sions of de-light re-veal-ing,

Loo _____ Loo loo loo loo.

Moth - er, here, her watch is keep-ing   all   thro' the night.
Breathes a pure and ho - ly feel-ing   all   thro' the night.

Simple descants are included in most of the basic music
series and also may be located in various other books.[4] When

[3] From *Music for Young Americans*, Book Four, New York: American
Book Company, 1960, pp. 158-159. Used by permission.

[4] For suggested descant books, see the listing on pp. 226-27.

the teacher understands the harmonic structure underlying a particular song, it will be found relatively easy for him to devise descants to meet the interests and needs of a particular class.

Rounds and canons

Rounds and canons are a form of musical imitation in which each of two or more parts enter in successive order. A round repeats back to the beginning and the point of imitation is always at the unison (rounds are sometimes called "circle canons"). A canon does not repeat and the point of imitation may be at the unison or at any other interval. Both are valuable in that they may provide a relatively easy and satisfying musical experience in which singers have the opportunity to hear the "interplay" of one part against another. A feeling for harmony may thus be developed and a degree of independency for singing a different vocal line may result.

Children's success in singing rounds and canons is dependent, to a large extent, upon their familiarity with the "tune," and their ability to "hold" their respective parts. After children have had considerable experience, they will enjoy singing rounds in three or more parts; however, initially it is suggested that they be limited to two parts. Following are some approaches to teaching rounds and canons in two parts.

1. The children may sing one part while the teacher sings the other.
2. One group may sing their part, while the other plays their part on one of the simple wind instruments.
3. Both groups may play their parts on simple wind instruments (or a combination of instruments may be used), including melody bells, piano, and simple wind instruments.
4. Two groups of rhythm or percussion instruments, each with a contrasting tonal quality, may be used. This approach, with each group playing the rhythm of the melody, brings out the rhythmic interplay of the parts.
5. Both groups may sing their respective parts.

At all times the teacher should make certain that the children know the melody sufficiently well before dividing them into singing groups, and that each group listens not only to themselves but to the other voices as well. Benefit will be gained from singing rounds and canons only to the extent that children listen to the relationship between their part and the others.

"Lovely Evening" and "Old Texas" are examples of a round and a canon respectively that when sung in a smooth, flowing manner enable a child to sense more readily the relationship of his part to the others. It is suggested, for this reason, that a number of this type be included, particularly in the children's early experiences with rounds and canons.

Lovely Evening

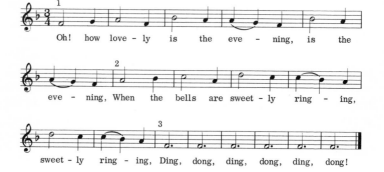

Old Texas [6]

[6] From *Music In Our Country*, © 1962, Morristown, N.J.: Silver Burdett Company. Used by permission.

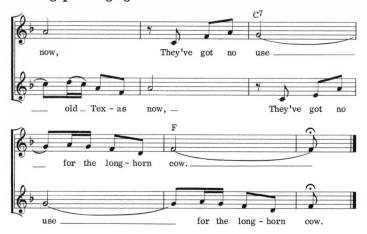

The Australian round "Kookaburra," and the canon "The Alphabet" are sung in a more detached style and are particularly enjoyable to children because of their humorous character. Many rounds and canons of this type should also be included in the children's repertoire.

Kookaburra [5]

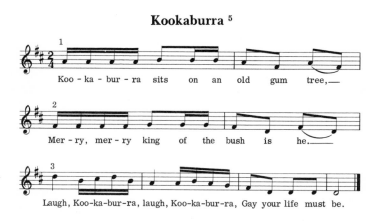

[5] From *The Ditty Bag* by Janet E. Tobitt, Pleasantville, N.Y., 1946. Used by permission.

The Alphabet [7]

Rounds and canons may be introduced to children as early as the third grade. Particular emphasis on them should occur at the fourth grade level, with continuing experience in grades five and six. A number of rounds and canons may be found in the basic music series for grades 4-6, and a listing of some other sources is included at the end of this chapter.

Combined songs

The value of singing combined songs, *i.e.,* two different songs simultaneously, is primarily recreational; however, the

[7] From *Rounds and Canons,* Harry R. Wilson. Used by permission of the publishers, Schmitt, Hall & McCreary Company, Minneapolis, Minn.

activity does contribute in some degree to the development of a feeling for harmony when it is a cooperative rather than competitive affair. Before singing combined songs, the teacher should make sure that the class knows each song reasonably well and that they understand the importance of listening carefully to the other group as well as to their own. Following are a number of suggested songs which may be effectively combined, either with voices, instruments, or a combination of both.[8]

"Are You Sleeping"	"Three Blind Mice"
"The Farmer in the Dell"	"Three Blind Mice"
"Keep the Home Fires Burning"	"The Long, Long Trail"
"Old Folks at Home"	"Humoresque"
"Row, Row Your Boat"	"Three Blind Mice"
"Solomon Levi"	"The Spanish Cavalier"
"Ten Little Indians"	"Skip to My Lou"
"Tipperary"	"Pack up your Troubles"

Harmonizing song endings

Harmonizing the final cadence of a song sung in unison can enhance the singing of it as well as develop interest in harmony that will lead to further experiences in part-singing. After selecting an appropriate song, the teacher may teach by rote either a two or three-part harmonization of the final cadence. Initially, it is desirable to make the harmonizations as simple as possible and to present the cadence in only two parts. For example, the final two measures in "America" might be sung as follows:

As students gain experience in this activity they may be encouraged to attempt to harmonize by ear their own song end-

---

8 For a variety of other combined songs, see Frederick Beckman, *Partner Songs* (1958), and *More Partner Songs* (1962), Boston: Ginn and Company.

ings. With the guidance of the teacher they should also endeavor to notate the parts on the chalkboard. This experience may lead the group to an examination of the endings of various two-part songs. In many they will observe that the last two pitches of the upper, or soprano, part is often either *re, do,* or *ti, do,* and that the pitches in the lower, or alto, part may often be identified as *sol, do,* or *fa, mi.* From analyzing a number of songs the students will be better prepared to harmonize and subsequently notate endings for other songs.

After varied experiences with two-part singing, the teacher may suggest that the class harmonize certain song endings in three, rather than two parts. For example, the following version of the final cadence of the familiar song "All Through the Night" may be used in preparation for three-part singing.

Singing chord roots

As the root of a chord is fundamental and the easiest part of the chord to hear, the singing of chord roots is an excellent experience for children in the intermediate grades. Initially, the teacher, as a means of introducing the procedure, may sing or play the chord roots on the piano, while the class sings the song in unison. After briefly discussing with the class what he did, the teacher may ask the class to write the syllable names of the chord roots under the text of the song.[9] (Generally one syllable for each measure is adequate.) The entire class may then sing the syllables as the teacher plays the melody on the piano or some other instrument. After this a variety of approaches are possible. The class may divide into two equal groups: one may

[9] Some basic series already have the syllables written in for certain selected songs. Thus, in the initial presentation, the teacher need only call the class' attention to them and ask the class to follow in their books while he plays or sings them.

sing the chord roots with syllables while the other group sings the melody of the song, or a group of instruments may play the melody while most of the class sings the syllables.

Harmonizing "by ear"

As students gain a gradual feeling for harmony and the relationship of one part to another, they will enjoy harmonizing familiar songs by ear. This is highly important to the development of the aural sense. The teacher should utilize harmonizing in the classroom and should also encourage the children to practice it whenever the opportunity provides itself (for example, at Boy and Girl Scout sings). Students who develop the ability to harmonize songs "by ear" will learn more readily to translate the printed symbols on the page into actual harmony.

Songs should be selected for the initial experiences that have a minimum of chord changes. For example, in the song "Oh Where Has My Little Dog Gone?" an effective second part may be achieved through singing the pitches *do, sol,* and at the final cadence *sol, la, ti, do.* This approach to harmonizing obviously grows out of the experience of singing chord roots and simulates a bass part (even though the voices are unchanged). Teachers will also want to help children create an alto part, using largely thirds and sixths, with other intervals as passing tones.

After a reasonable amount of experience in harmonizing songs by ear, the class should endeavor, with teacher guidance and assistance, to properly notate the harmonization of their second parts.

Singing chordal accompaniments

The singing of chordal accompaniments to a familiar song is not only an enjoyable and satisfying musical activity, but is an excellent preparatory experience to the singing of three-part songs. This activity may be introduced at the fifth grade level.

The following chord progression may be written on the chalkboard, and each of three previously determined groups asked to first identify and then sing the syllables in their part. In this particular case, it generally is best for each group to sing their part separately. Next, the teacher may give the pitches for the first chord and then ask the class to sing each chord as he points to it.

	I	IV	V⁷	I
1st part:	do,	do,	ti,	do.
2nd part:	sol,	la,	sol,	sol.
3rd part:	mi,	fa,	fa,	mi.

As chords in a song will not occur in the precise order as the sequence written on the chalkboard, the teacher should then have the class sing a progression in varying sequences. It is also desirable in this practice to prescribe a certain meter and establish a particular tempo. The following chord progression might be sung by the class as he points to the three basic chords written on the chalkboard: I, I, IV, I, I, I, V⁷, I.

After the class has had a reasonable amount of experience in singing chord progressions in this manner, they may then be used as accompaniment for particular selected songs. The song melody may be played on an instrument, or a small group of selected students may be asked to sing it. The teacher may use one of several procedures. He may point to the appropriate chord on the chalkboard, to the column of syllables under the chords, or he may indicate the appropriate chord by holding up one, four, or five fingers—each signal representing a particular chord.

Initial experiences in part-singing

Two-part songs are generally introduced to children on the fifth grade level. Students who have had the advantage of preparatory aural experiences with harmony will be more likely to be successful in their first attempts at part-singing. Without a minimum degree of adequate preparation, students will find the task more difficult than it needs to be; frustration will result, and the teacher will often resort to the outmoded procedure of teaching only one part at a time and of eventually combining them.

In presenting two-part songs to children for the first time, the teacher should endeavor to bring to bear all their previous understandings and experiences upon the new learning activity. First, the teacher should call the class' attention to the score and then ask them in what way it looks different from other songs they have sung. After the group observes that there are two vocal lines rather than one, the teacher may need to explain that in some instances both parts sing the same pitch. The pitch is indicated by only one notehead with two stems—up for the soprano and down for the alto $\left(\rho \right)$. In most simple two-part songs, involving largely thirds and sixths and the same rhythmic pattern, the stems for both noteheads will be in one direction. This is the case except where the two parts are rhythmically different; then the stems on the noteheads for the lower part will point downward, while those for the upper part will point upward, as in the example below.

In a few songs encountered it will be noted that *all* the stems for the soprano part are up and those for the alto part down. It is well for the teacher to point out these differences immediately before the song is introduced.

While adequate preparatory experiences prior to part-singing will facilitate the learning process, the initial attempt will be less frustrating to the children if the teacher does utilize a semi-rote procedure. Such a procedure should be used until the children possess a certain degree of familiarity with part-songs and an ability to read the songs with a minimum degree of teacher assistance. This suggested procedure can be outlined as follows.

1. The teacher plays both parts on the piano, while the class listens and follows the score.
2. The students and the teacher both sing the second part, while the teacher plays both parts on the piano.
3. The class sings the second part, while the teacher sings the first part and plays both parts on the piano.
4. The high voices sing the soprano part and the low voices the alto part. (The teacher should assist the group that needs help the most.)

In general, several basic reasons exist for this process and should be given due consideration by the teacher. First, it is often desirable, in introducing new music, to provide the class with an overall view before they attempt to sing the parts (*i.e., what the music sounds like* and *what it looks like*). This factor is highly important and should be considered unless the purpose of the lesson is only to develop increased skills in music reading. Secondly, the vocal line of the alto part is often less "melodious," somewhat more elusive, and generally a little more difficult to learn, especially when the class is familiar with the melodic part. Therefore, it is suggested that the class begin by singing first the alto or second part. This part is not learned in isolation, however, but in its relationship to the soprano part which is also played simultaneously on the piano. Finally, before the children are divided for the purpose of singing their respective parts, it is desirable for them to have the experience of the teacher singing one part while they sing the other. The teacher is best able to sing at a dynamic level which will provide a pleasing harmonic effect, yet will not "pull" the students away from the part they are singing. Dividing the voices into two groups assumes that the teacher knows the voice classification of each individual student and has previously divided the class according to parts or into high and low voices. If this has not been done, then the class may be divided arbitrarily according to left and right sides of the room.

Regardless of whether or not the voices have previously been classified according to high and low voices, it is desirable for all the students to have some experience in singing both the soprano and alto parts. Therefore, in the above procedure a fifth step might be added, namely, to ask the two groups to periodically switch parts. Experience in singing both parts helps to develop a greater awareness of the part being harmonized with, and more careful listening habits and cooperative endeavor is thus facilitated.

Improving part-singing

How does the teacher increase a class' skill in part singing? Certainly not by a mere repetition of the previously mentioned semi-rote process, but by utilizing all available means to help the students to interpret the printed symbols more accurately. Children should be helped to relate their aural experiences to the harmonic notation; they should observe what the music they have sung *looks* like and, based upon such experiences, try to determine what similar harmonic notation in unfamiliar songs *sounds* like. Broad experiences of this type are essential to the development of increased skill in part singing.

Developing an increased understanding of harmonic notation, and of how it sounds the way it does, will contribute to the children's musical development. A knowledge of intervals, and of what they *sound* and *look* like is a good beginning point. It is helpful for a class to devote some time to analyzing the intervals in selected part songs. The teacher might ask the class to examine a new song and identify the most frequently occurring intervals (probably thirds and/or sixths). Perhaps later he will ask the class to identify the intervals resulting when the voice parts move from an interval of a sixth to that of a third. Subsequently, the teacher may select a particular song and ask the class if they can remember what the intervals in the first phrase sound like. Assuming, for example, that the harmony is comprised simply of thirds, he will give the lower part its pitch and ask the higher voices to sing their beginning pitch. The procedure may then be reversed. Eventually all intervals should be identified and sung in this manner. It is, of course, helpful and necessary for the teacher to guide the class carefully in understanding the sound of particular notation. However, a word of caution! Too much time devoted to this procedure can result in boredom. Such analytical procedures should never be a tedious process, but should be approached as an exciting discovery. The activity should always be meaningful and related to music that the class is learning, never an abstract experience unrelated to actual music.

In addition to analyzing and singing various intervals, the teacher will also find it highly profitable to use a creative approach in studying harmonic notation. He may begin by asking the class to harmonize by ear a particular favorite song. Then the class, with the teacher's help, will endeavor to notate the "newly created" harmonization on the chalkboard. A discussion of the intervals used and why the song sounds the way it does will contribute substantially to improving eye-ear relationships. To provide further motivation, and for later study, the song should be duplicated and a copy distributed to each student in order that he may "possess" a record of the group's creative efforts.

In addition to the study of harmonic notation, there should be continual emphasis upon varied activities designed to improve music reading in general.

The children should identify the meter and tonality of the song. Before even attempting to read a new song, students should be asked to observe the meter signature to see if the music swings in two's or in three's. Some physical response to pulsation and accent is helpful—such as marking out the pulsation (through rapping, tapping, or clapping) and accenting the strong beats in each measure. The class should also determine the tonality of the song by first locating *do* (or *la*) and then comparing this pitch with the beginning and ending pitches to see if the song is in major or minor tonality. The class may then determine and sing the syllables of the notes in the first measure (or the first phrase) to establish the tonality of the song.

Students should also be asked to scan the music and look for similarities and differences in the notation of various phrases. For example, the teacher may ask the class to examine the first phrase carefully, and then to look for other phrases that are either identical, only slightly different, or completely different. A discussion should then follow in regard to these similarities and differences. For an analysis of specifics on the printed page, the teacher may ask the class to identify certain harmonic patterns in the music. The teacher may specify a particular measure or pattern and ask the class to identify and frame a similar pattern. Or, if the pattern is quite repetitious, to count the number of such patterns in the music. A variation of this procedure is for the teacher to play on the piano a particular pattern (or phrase) and ask the class to locate it in their music. This procedure, and other variations of it, also helps to strengthen eye-ear relationships.

Through all these analytical experiences students may be helped to learn to read harmonic notation. The experience of recognizing various patterns in a wide variety of songs and different circumstances is necessary to the development of increased skill in part-singing.

Topics for discussion

1. Endeavor to recall your early experiences with part-singing. Through what means did the teacher create a feeling of anticipation for engaging in this new type of activity?

2. Outline a variety of types of musical experience necessary and desirable as preparation for the undertaking of part-singing in the fifth grade. Why are these activities and experiences important?

3. Why should a rote approach to the teaching of part-singing be avoided and to what extent can this objective be realized?

4. What type of experiences lead to the development of independency in music reading and part-singing? What factors cause some singers to be overly dependent upon others?

Suggestions for further study

ELLIOTT, Raymond. "First Experiences in Part-Singing," *Music Education in Action: Basic Principles and Practical Methods*. Edited by Archie N. Jones. Boston: Allyn and Bacon, 1960, pp. 44-47.

GARRETSON, Robert L. *Conducting Choral Music*. Second Edition. Boston: Allyn and Bacon, 1965, Chapter 5.

KODÁLY, Zoltán. *Choral Method: Let Us Sing Correctly*. London: Boosey & Hawkes, Inc., 1952.

NYE, Robert and NYE, Vernice T. *Music in the Elementary School*, 2nd edition. Englewood Cliffs, N.J.: Prentice-Hall, 1957, 1964, Chapter Seven.

Suggested materials

ANDERSON, Ruth. *Rounds from Many Countries*. New York: G. Schirmer, Inc., 1961.

BECKMAN, Frederick. *Partner Songs* (1958); *More Partner Songs* (1962). Boston: Ginn and Company.

DANIEL, Oliver. *Round and Round and Round They Go*. Evanston, Ill.: Summy-Birchard Publishing Company, 1952.

DRAKE, Janet. *The Descant Program Book*. Rockville Centre, N.Y.: Belwin, Inc., 1957.

DUNNING, Sarah L. *Fifty-five Rounds and Canons*. New York: G. Schirmer, Inc., 1936.

FOLTZ, David, and MURPHY, Arthur. *Descants to Sing for Fun.* New York: Mills Music, Inc.

KODÁLY, Zoltán. *Choral Method: Let Us Sing Correctly.* London: Boosey & Hawkes, 1952.

KRONE, Beatrice, and KRONE, Max. *Our First Songs to Sing With Descants* (1949); *Very Easy Descants* (1951); *Songs to Sing with Descants* (1940); *Descants for Christmas* (1949); *Our Third Book of Descants,* Revised (1954); *From Descants to Trios,* Revised (1954); *Intermediate Descants* (1954); *Descants and Rounds for Special Days* (1962). Park Ridge, Ill.: Neil A. Kjos Music Company.

NEWMAN, Harold. *Round and Round Again: 50 Canons and Rounds.* New York: Hargail Music Press, 1965.

TAYLOR, Mary Catherine, WINDHAM, Margarita, and SIMPSON, Claude. *Catch That Catch Can* (One Hundred English Rounds and Catches). Boston: E. C. Schirmer Music Company, 1945 (3 parts—advanced).

TERRI, Salli. *Rounds for Everyone from Everywhere.* New York: Lawson Gould Music Publishers, Inc., 1961.

WILSON, Harry R. *Rounds and Canons.* Minneapolis: Schmitt, Hall & McCreary, 1943.

All Basic Music Series. For listing of books and publishers, see the Appendix, pp. 252-55.

Films

Harmony In Music (Coronet Instructional Films, 65 E. South Water St., Chicago, Ill.), 1957, b&w or color, 13½ min. Elem./Col.

Two-Part Singing (Johnston Hunt Productions, 6509 De Longpre Ave., Hollywood, Calif.), 1951, b&w, 19 min. Elem./Col.

9 Organizing the learning experience

It is essential that teachers give thoughtful consideration to the planning and organization of classroom learning experiences. Clear-cut goals are, first of all, an absolute necessity. They provide a basis for the accomplishment of a higher level of musical understanding and skills. In education today the stress is upon the *quality* of the educational experience. Such experiences are not likely to occur when teachers engage in haphazard planning and improvisation on a day-to-day basis.

In our changing world, the selection of appropriate curriculum content is a continuing problem for educators. With the vast array of musical literature contained by our heritage, the selection of appropriate experiences then presents no less of a problem to educators than does the other curricular areas. The teacher must consider the needs, interests, and abilities of his particular group of children if the selected materials are to be meaningful. He must also consider the *variety* and *breadth* of the musical experiences. All the avenues of musical experience—singing, playing, listening, bodily movement, and creative activities—generally cannot be presented on a given day. When such a wide range of activities is included in an educational program, there is always the danger that some aspects will be treated in a superficial manner rather than in a depth sufficient enough to foster continuous musical growth. Careful planning, then, is of paramount importance if these problems are to be minimized.

228

Unit teaching

Many teachers have concluded that students learn more effectively through unit teaching—in which the presentation of concepts, facts, skills, and attitudes, is related to some major topic, question, or problem—than they do from the day-to-day presentation of unrelated and isolated bits of information. The unit approach to teaching involves the organization of the material of a course into a series of subdivisions, each of which is based upon a major topic, area, or problem. Units may range in length from between two to six weeks, depending on the significance of the topic and the maturity and receptiveness of the children.

Students both learn and retain information better when they can relate it to a larger whole. Unit teaching is, therefore, a far more effective teaching procedure than is the traditional approach where little attempt is made to tie information together or relate it to work taught in other classes.[1]

Music and the social studies

Various approaches exist for organizing curricular content. Perhaps the most widely known is the correlation of all curricular areas, including music, with some central topic growing out of the social studies. This approach generally cuts across traditional subject matter lines, and is illustrated as follows by the topic of "Mexico," generally undertaken in the fourth grade.[2]

Social studies. This constitutes perhaps the core of the subject matter to be studied; the student would study about the

[1] For a detailed discussion of Unit Teaching, see Ralph L. Pounds and Robert L. Garretson, *Principles of Modern Education,* New York: The Macmillan Company, 1962, Ch. 9.

[2] *Ibid.,* p. 243.

lives of the Mexican people and their customs, and the geography, natural resources, and products of Mexico.

Language arts.   A study of Mexican folk lore and literature adaptable to the children's level may be studied. The class might write a story about Mexican customs or life in Mexico. Stories about Mexican life could be read and studied in class.

Music.   Folk songs from Mexico may be sung and accompanied by Latin-American instruments. Typical rhythmic figures may be analyzed and new patterns created for song accompaniment purposes. Children might listen to recordings of Mexican music and discuss its unique characteristics.

Art.   A study could be made of the various forms of Mexican art—baskets could be woven, pottery made, and pictures depicting life in Mexico may be drawn.

Physical education.   The class could learn and participate in the games and folk dances of Mexico.

Arithmetic.   Although it is not necessary nor feasible to include all of the arithmetic work as a part of an integrated experience unit, in many instances teachers can provide worthwhile arithmetic experiences in connection with one of these units. If the teacher desires to include such experiences, the class could, for example, learn to count in Spanish, and learn the various coin values. Certain problems in the basic arithmetic text could be adapted by simply changing the names and places in the problems. Thus, some of the skill objectives of arithmetic may be achieved, while at the same time the material is made more meaningful by adapting it to the broad topic being studied.[3]

One of the central objectives of education today is the development of an understanding of other peoples and their culture. While the social studies and language arts form the core of this unit teaching approach, it can be readily seen that the study of any culture would not be complete, or seen in its truest perspective, if, for example, the music, the art, and the folk dances

[3] *Ibid.,* p. 243.

were not included. For through music, in particular, the hopes, fears, aspirations, and attitudes of the people are often expressed.

The preceding integrated teaching approach may be best utilized by classroom teachers who are cognizant of the relationships between the subject matter areas and the all-encompassing unit topic. With social studies and language arts serving as the basic core of the unit there is, however, the ever-present danger that the music may be dealt with somewhat superficially. Music must never be treated in an incidental manner, but dealt with in a degree of depth sufficient to develop basic understandings and skills. As previously indicated, it is generally accepted that while, for example, some aspects of mathematics may be correlated with a unit topic, this subject must be dealt with separately if the concepts involved in the new mathematics are to be adequately comprehended by children. Music study, on the other hand, may be entirely interwoven into the fabric of the social studies unit, *or* it may be undertaken at a later period in the day, with the arrangement depending on a block of time sufficient in length to accomplish the desired musical objectives.

Following are some specific suggestions for the teaching of music in connection with a unit on Mexico.

Singing

1. Discuss the meaning of the song text as it relates to understanding the Mexican people.
2. Identify the meter and key of the song.
3. Teach tone quality and diction appropriate to the style of the song.
4. Analyze the phrase structure of the song, look for identical, similar, and different phrases.
5. Identify melodic fragments or tonal patterns that reveal the character of the song.

Rhythmic activities

1. Analyze the rhythmic patterns in songs.
2. Clap and/or tap the predominant rhythmic patterns.
3. Create and notate on the chalkboard various rhythmic patterns to accompany the singing of songs, using such

Latin-American instruments as claves, maracas, guiro, tubos, Conga drum, and Bongo drums.

Listening

1. Listen to the interpretation of Mexican folk songs as performed by various groups.
2. Listen to composed music, such as *El Salon Mexico* by Aaron Copland, and follow with a discussion of the idiom in which the music was written and of perhaps some of the more obvious compositional devices the composer employed, such as particular tonal patterns and rhythmic figures.

Creating

1. Ask the children to write additional verses to a familiar song.
2. Write a poem on some aspect of Mexican life and set it to music.
3. Construct some Latin-American instruments.

While this teaching approach, in which music is correlated with the social studies, is used primarily by classroom teachers, there are many special music teachers, functioning in a departmentalized system, who endeavor to coordinate their teaching with the on-going activities of the classroom teachers. When a given fifth grade class is, for example, involved in a study of the topic, "The Westward Movement," then the special music teacher will often select and concentrate upon the music of this period. Such an approach is highly desirable because the music teacher is able to capitalize upon the children's interest in the topic created by the classroom teacher. Some music teachers decry this approach with a comment such as, "My task is to teach music, not social studies!" This may be true. But if the specific objective for a particular lesson is, for example, "to clarify the children's understanding of the dotted note," there is no reason to believe that it cannot be accomplished just as well through the teaching of a folk song related to a unit topic as it can through one totally unrelated to the social studies unit. All that is really needed is adequate planning and careful selection of appropriate songs or music materials. In the selection of appropriate music, whether by the classroom teacher or the special music teacher, good judgment should always be used. When folk music is being considered, it should be selected on the basis of its musical value and its authenticity—that is, the music should be a genuine expression of the thoughts, attitudes, and beliefs of the people it represents. Correlating music with the social studies by some superficial means, for example, on the basis of a song title only rather than on the authenticity of the music, is an unjustifiable practice. It defeats the purpose of correlation and is generally a waste of time.

Organizing music units

With the objective in mind of developing musical understanding, a good many music teachers prefer to organize their teaching units around some central topic where the stress is upon music itself, rather than the social studies. In practice, varied approaches may be observed. Some teachers organize their units on such topics as, "Music in the Colonial Period," or "Music of the Civil War," and other similar topics. While in this approach the stress is primarily on the music, concepts emanating from the social studies are not necessarily ignored, but are related whenever desirable to improve musical understanding.

While some teachers present these unit topics to children without regard to the on-going activities in the students' other classes, many endeavor to cover these topics during the same general period that related topics are being taught in the social studies classes. While the presentation of specific social studies units will vary from school to school, the following music units will generally parallel the work undertaken at each of the grade levels.

Grade One—"Singing and Playing Together"

Grade Two—"Music in our Community"

Grade Three—"Music of the American Indian"
    "Music and Transportation"

Grade Four—"Music of Mexico"
               "Music in the Eastern Hemisphere" (China, Japan, the Philippines, etc.)
Grade Five—"Music of the Colonial Period"
               "Music of the Civil War"
               "Music of the Pioneers"
Grade Six—"Music of European Countries"
               (separate units may be planned on the music of England, France, Germany, Italy, Russia, etc.)

To organize units in the manner suggested above, teachers will necessarily need to plan their work carefully. Obviously, the most suitable teaching materials will not be found from one source, and are not likely to be identified on the spur of the moment. Therefore, it is suggested that teachers maintain a file into which appropriate and pertinent information and materials be inserted as they are located. After a sufficient amount of material has been collected it will be found helpful to organize it into a "resource unit," which may be defined as a broad compilation of materials related to a particular topic and appropriate to a limited range of age levels (not more than three years).

A music resource unit, to be of maximum value and benefit, should include the following.

Outline of a Music Resource Unit

   I. Objectives of the Unit
      A. General
      B. Specific
  II. Music Materials and Activities
      A. Songs
         1. Title and source (book series, publisher, and page number)
         2. Suggestions for teaching
      B. Rhythmic Activities
         1. Interpretive and patterned responses
         2. Singing games and folk dances, including source
      C. Recordings
         1. Title, performing group, recording company and record number.

2. Suggestions for "guided listening"
D. Instruments
   1. Music materials and source
   2. Suggested procedures
E. Creative Activities
   1. Suggestions for appropriate group activities
   2. Individual activities
F. Music Reading
   1. Materials selected for reading purposes, including source
   2. Procedures for improving skills
III. Related Materials, Resources and Activities
   A. Pictures of composers, performing organizations, musical instruments, etc.
   B. Locations for suitable field trips.
   C. Resource persons in the community, specialists in a particular area who might be brought to the classroom to present information on a specific related topic
   D. Supplementary reading materials appropriate to the level of a particular group of children (books and pamphlets)
   E. Newspaper and magazine articles pertaining to the topic
   F. Bibliography of books and source materials for teachers
   G. Educational films pertaining to the topic
IV. Suggested Culminating Activities
   A. Procedures for reviewing and summarizing the work covered during the unit
   B. Music programs presented for other classes on the same grade level, or for an all-school assembly
V. Suggested Evaluative Procedures
   A. Informal discussion
   B. Individual and/or group reports
   C. Check lists and scales for measuring interests and attitudes
   D. Written examinations
   E. Student self-evaluation, with questions, such as,

"Did we accomplish what we set out to learn?" and
"Would you like to undertake a similar study in
the same, or in a different way?" "What procedures
would you suggest?"

A vast improvement has occurred in recent years in the
basic song texts designed for use in elementary schools. One of
the more significant changes has been the inclusion of varied
techniques for improving musicality, such as, for example, suggestions for instrumental accompaniment (Latin-American instruments, melody bells, resonator bells, autoharps, etc.). Teacher's
books for these basic series offer more concrete and specific suggestions for implementing the program than ever before. Perhaps these changes only reflect the growing seriousness with
which the music educator approaches his task.

A rather substantially large group of music educators prefer to organize their teaching around the principal objective of
developing an understanding of the various elements of music,
i.e., melody, rhythm, harmony, form and tone color.[4] Such
an approach would involve the organization of musical activities to cover the entire year rather than only a portion of it.
The all-encompassing unit topic in this case might simply be
"Understanding Music," or "Music in Our Lives," with the
underlying unifying structure being the basic elements of music
(melody, rhythm, harmony, form, and tone color). While each
of these elements may be dealt with separately in particular
lessons, their interrelationships will serve as the basis for a
considerable number of other lessons.

Another approach would be to organize shorter sub-units—
varying in length from a few days to two weeks—around each of
these elements of music. As the students increase their insights
into the inner-workings of music these recurring topics may build
upon themselves, developing increased understanding each time
they are presented.

4 For a guide to the study of music elements, with objectives for each
grade level, see the Teachers Editions of the basic series *Making Music Your
Own,* Morristown, N.J.: Silver Burdett Company, 1965. See also the Teacher's
Editions of *Growing With Music,* Englewood Cliffs, N.J.: Prentice-Hall, Inc.,
1963.

As previously indicated, varied approaches to the teaching of music exist today and for teachers to express a preference for one over another is to be expected. Some teachers, however, have found an "eclectic" approach, in which the stronger points of varying approaches are adapted into their teaching procedure, to be the most suitable for their purposes. Regardless of the manner in which the teacher organizes his material, the important thing is that he does organize. One of the deterrents to the improvement of music education has been the casual, "shooting from the hip" approach, which is inimical to the best interests of the students.

Developing lesson plans

The critical area in the educative process is the point where *teacher meets pupil.* For the quality of this learning experience to be what it hopefully should be, it is necessary that the teacher give careful consideration to the planning of each lesson. It is essential, of course, that teachers prepare written plans—for writing serves to clarify one's thinking and provides a more objective look at the continuity and balance of a lesson.

The beginning point in the preparation of any lesson plan is the determination of objectives. Presumably the general or long-term objectives have been given consideration in the preparation of the teaching unit. The specific objectives, or what the teacher hopes to accomplish on a given day, must also be carefully formulated, as they not only serve as a guide for developing the structure of the lesson but as criteria for the evaluation of the effectiveness of the lesson after it has been taught.[5]

The next step is the selection of the materials and activities to best meet these objectives. In this process, consideration must be given to the needs, interests, and musical backgrounds of the children. When objectives have been carefully considered, then teachers will realize the folly of planning and teaching the same lesson to different classes of varying grade levels. The integrated

[5] For examples of general and specific objectives, see pp. 7-9.

lesson, in which *all* the activities are related and are chosen to fulfill a specific objective or objectives, is a necessary and essential procedure in planning for maximum musical growth. If, for example, the teacher's objective is "to develop an increased understanding of syncopation in music," then all activities should be directed toward improving comprehension of this concept (see Lesson Plan 2). Furthermore, the sequence of activities in the integrated lesson is more readily understood by students, and their resistance to "teacher-imposed" activities is likely to be less, when they see continuity than when activities are seemingly unrelated.

The amount of time devoted to each aspect of the lesson, determined primarily by the amount of time available, must also be considered. In the five-fold program of music education, experiences in singing, rhythmic activities, listening, instrumental study, and creative activities can usually not all be included in one lesson. The teacher must necessarily choose and select those activities that will best fulfill the objectives of the lesson. Of course, activities not included in one lesson should be included in subsequent lessons. The pacing of the lesson is also highly important. One problem, particularly with beginning teachers, is that of devoting too much time to one or two activities, neglecting or excluding completely the others planned for the lesson. This pitfall can sometimes be avoided if a specific amount of time is planned for each activity, and if the teacher then disciplines himself to follow this plan.

The following sample lesson on "Bells" is designed for the first grade and might well grow out of a teaching unit on "Exploring Our Musical World," which is appropriate to the general objectives for this age group.

Lesson Plan No. 1 on "Bells" (for First Grade)

I. Objectives
   A. To develop an awareness of the varying pitches and characteristics of bell-like sounds heard in everyday life.
   B. To motivate the children toward further experimentation of the unique tonal characteristics of various materials.

2. Tune three water glasses to the pitches D, E, and F♯.
   a. Strike the glasses gently with a metal beater.
   b. Point out the pitch changes as the water is poured.
3. Sing a simple song involving only three pitches, *e.g.,* "Hot Cross Buns."
   a. Teacher plays while children sing.
   b. Allow several children the opportunity to play the "glass bells."
4. Experiment with sounds of other materials (depending on time available).
   a. Different lengths of nails suspended on strings.
   b. Different sizes of bottles filled with varying amounts of water.
   c. Different sizes of flower pots.
   d. Encourage children to experiment at home with other materials.

Lesson Plan No. 2 on "Syncopation" (for Fifth Grade)

I. Objectives
   A. To develop a feeling for syncopation and the ability to recognize it in notation, and to encourage correct rhythmic response.
   B. To develop further insight into the intricacies of rhythm by encouraging the class to create their own rhythmic patterns.
II. Activities
   A. Singing, Rhythmic Response, Playing Instruments, and Creative Activities
      (Song—"This Train" (Negro Folk Song) *Music for Young Americans*, Book Five, p. 95.)
      1. Present song, while class follows the notation and the text in their books.
      2. Ask class to identify the mood (happy and carefree) by carefully examining the text of the song.
      3. Have class sing as the teacher accompanies with piano.

Organizing the learning experience

II. Activities

    A. Singing, Rhythmic Response, and Tone M
       (Song—"Bells," *The American Singer*, Boo
       p. 179).

       1. Motivation—through questioning. "Who
          me about the different kinds of bells th
          heard?"

       2. Teach song by rote (whole song method

       3. Select and instruct students to "pull do
          on the bell rope" in the second phrase (
          in each measure).

       4. Tone matching—Teacher imitates the bel

Ding – dong

              and designated children res
      the "echo."

    B. Listening
      (Recording—"Legend of the Bells" from *Ch
      Normandy* by Planquette, RCA Listening A
      Volume 1, E77.)

      "The melody is from a song in the operetta,
      of Normandy. The story tells us about an ol
      that had been deserted for many years. It w
      that whenever the owner or one of his heirs re
      the chimes in the tower would ring out,
      everyone would know. The music tells us h
      chimes would sound."

      "Listen for the high pitched, fast sounding
      which play the melody, and the lower, slower
      which ring only now and then or once in a w

    C. Playing and Exploratory Activities

       1. Have children tell about their experienc
          bells and bell sounds (optional—dependi
          available time).

[6] Lilla Belle Pitts and Gladys Tipton, *Notes for Teachers*, RCA
ing Activities, Volume 1, E 77, pp. 2-3.

4. Ask class to identify the predominant rhythmic pattern

$$\left(\text{♪}\underset{>}{\text{♩}} \quad \text{♪}\text{♫} \quad \text{♫} \right)$$

5. Write the pattern on the chalkboard.
6. Have the class clap the pattern together.
7. "What effect does this rhythmic pattern create?" (Excitement)
8. Explain that this effect occurs when the stress is "off the beat," which is not normally expected, and is called "syncopation."
9. Select several students to accompany the singing with instruments such as claves, guiro, drums by playing the pattern:

10. Encourage students to create other rhythmic patterns to accompany the singing. Hopefully a pattern might be taught such as:

11. Combine various suggestions to make a rhythm orchestration to accompany the song. For example:

B. Listening and Playing
   (Recording—"Danza" from *Brazilian Impressions* by
   Ottorino Respighi, *Adventures in Music,* Grade 5,
   Volume 2, RCA Victor.)
   1. Give background information on composer (see
      Teacher's Guide, pp. 12-13).
   2. Ask class to listen and describe the mood.
   3. Write on chalkboard, and ask the class to listen
      for, the syncopated figures.

   Differentiate between the "slower" and "quicker
   moving" syncopated figures.
   4. Have the class clap or tap the patterns.
C. Singing and Rhythmic Study
   (Song—"Erie Canal," *Music in Our Country,* Book
   Five, pp. 94-95).
   1. Call attention to the syncopated figures in meas-
      ures one and two.

   2. Have class clap or tap the rhythmic pattern.
   3. Ask class to identify the total number of measures
      with a syncopated figure (nine).
   4. Sing the song (preferably with piano accom-
      paniment).
   5. Discuss the background or origin of the song be-
      fore singing it again.

Following the presentation of each daily lesson, the teacher
should evaluate its effectiveness. The questions should be asked,
"Did the children accomplish what I had hoped they would?"
and "What might I have done to improve the quality of the
learning experience?" This information will be found helpful in

planning subsequent lessons. In addition, marginal notes in answer to these questions may be made on the written plan itself, which should then be filed for future reference. The next time the lesson is taught these evaluative comments should prove helpful and, in addition to the insights gained in the interim period, the teacher will hopefully be able to further improve his teaching skills. Without the proper attention to these details—sometimes quite time consuming—music educators cannot hope to provide musical experiences of the type and quality which children so rightly deserve.

Topics for discussion

1. Discuss the effects of poor and haphazard planning upon the quality of the educative process.

2. What evidence does psychology present us in regard to the advantages of careful planning?

3. Discuss the advantages and disadvantages of correlating music with the social studies.

4. Discuss ways in which music may be correlated with such curricular areas as science, art, and physical education.

5. Prepare an extended list of topics for daily lessons suitable for a particular grade level.

6. Is it desirable to use only one basic lesson plan for several different classes each day?

7. Why is it desirable to evaluate the effectiveness of each lesson plan after it has been taught? What procedures would you use in the evaluative process?

8. Develop a unified lesson plan on a given topic for a particular group of children.

Suggestions for further study

MYERS, Louise K. *Teaching Children Music in the Elementary School.* Third Edition. Englewood Cliffs, N.J.: Prentice-Hall, Inc., 1961, Ch. 12.

NYE, Robert E., and NYE, Vernice T. *Music in the Elementary School.* Second Edition. Englewood Cliffs, N.J.: Prentice-Hall, Inc., 1964, Ch. 11.

PIERCE, Anne E. *Teaching Music in the Elementary School.* New York: Henry Holt and Company, 1959, Ch. 9.

POUNDS, Ralph L., and GARRETSON, Robert L. *Principles of Modern Education.* New York: The Macmillan Company, 1962, Ch. 9.

SWANSON, Bessie. *Music in the Education of Children.* Second Edition. Belmont, Calif.: Wadsworth Publishing Company, 1964, Ch. 9.

SWANSON, Bessie. *Planning Music in the Education of Children.* Belmont, Calif.: Wadsworth Publishing Company, 1965.

TIMMERMAN, Maurine. *Let's Teach Music.* Evanston, Illinois: Summy-Birchard Publishing Company, 1958, Ch. 7.

TOOZE, Ruth and KRONE, Beatrice Perham. *Literature and Music as Resources for Social Studies.* Englewood Cliffs, N.J.: Prentice-Hall, Inc., 1955.

Appendix

Bibliography

    1. Fundamentals of Music

    2. Music education: foundations, principles and methods

    3. General education: curriculum, principles and methods

Basic music textbooks

Addresses of music textbook publishers

Basic record series

Sources of catalogs of educational recordings

Sources of classroom instruments and equipment

Bibliography

Fundamentals of music

ANDREWS, J. Austin, and WARDIAN, Jeanne Foster, *Introduction to Music Fundamentals: A Programmed Textbook for the Elementary Classroom Teacher.* New York: Appleton-Century-Crofts, 1963.

BARNES, Robert A., *Fundamentals of Music: A Program of Self-Instruction.* New York: McGraw-Hill Book Company, 1964.

BENWARD, Bruce, *Sightsinging Complete.* Dubuque, Iowa: Wm. C. Brown Co. Publishers, 1965.

BERKOWITZ, Sol, FONTRIER, Gabriel, and KRAFT, Leo, *A New Approach to Sight Singing.* New York: W. W. Norton & Company, Inc., 1960.

CASS, Jeannette, *Rudiments of Music.* New York: Appleton-Century-Crofts, Inc., 1956.

CASTELLINI, John, *Rudiments of Music.* New York: W. W. Norton & Company, Inc., 1962.

CLOUGH, John, *Scales, Intervals, Keys, and Triads: A Self-Instruction Program.* New York: W. W. Norton & Company, Inc., 1964.

ELLIOT, Raymond, *Fundamentals of Music.* Second Edition. Englewood Cliffs, N.J.: Prentice-Hall, Inc., 1965.

ELLIOTT, Raymond, *Learning Music.* Columbus, Ohio: Charles E. Merrill Books, Inc., 1960.

FRACKENPOHL, Arthur, *Harmonization at the Piano.* Dubuque, Iowa: Wm. C. Brown Company Publishers, 1962.

HURD, Lyman C., and SAVAGE, Edith J., *First Experiences In Music.* Belmont, California: Wadsworth Publishing Company, 1966.

KNUTH, Alice Snyder, and KNUTH, William E., *Basic Resources for Learning Music.* Belmont, California: Wadsworth Publishing Company, 1966.

LEONHARD, Charles, *A Song Approach to Music Reading.* Morristown, New Jersey: Silver Burdett Company, 1953.

NYE, Robert E., and BERGETHON, Bjornar, *Basic Music for Class-room Teachers*. Second Edition. Englewood Cliffs, N.J.: Prentice-Hall, Inc., 1962.

PACE, Robert, *Music Essentials for Classroom Teachers*. San Francisco: Wadsworth Publishing Company, Inc., 1961.

POTTER, S. B., *Fundamentals of Music*. Mattapan, Mass.: Gamut Music Company, 1961.

SNYDER, Hartley D., *Fundamental Musicianship for the Class-room Teacher*. Third Edition. San Francisco: Fearon Publishers, 1959.

TMI-GROLIER, *Programmed Textbook: Fundamentals of Music*. New York: Teaching Machines, Inc., 1960.

WEYLAND, Rudolph H., *Learning to Read Music*. Dubuque, Iowa: Wm. C. Brown Company Publishers, 1961.

WILSON, Harry R. *Sing a Song at Sight*. Minneapolis: Schmitt; Hall & McCreary Company, 1954.

WINSLOW, Robert W., *Music Skills for Classroom Teachers*. Dubuque, Iowa: Wm. C. Brown Company Publishers, 1958.

WISLER, Gene C., *Music Fundamentals for the Classroom Teacher*. Boston: Allyn and Bacon, Inc., 1961.

Music education: foundations, principles and methods

ANDREWS, Gladys, *Creative Rhythmic Movement for Children*. Englewood Cliffs, N.J.: Prentice-Hall, Inc., 1954.

ANDREWS, Frances M., and COCKERILLE, Clara E., *Your School Music Program*. Englewood Cliffs, N.J.: Prentice-Hall, Inc., 1958.

BERGETHON, Bjonar and BOARDMAN, Eunice. *Musical Growth in the Elementary School*. New York: Holt, Rinehart and Winston, 1963.

BIRGE, Edward Bailey, *History of Public School Music in the United States*. Philadelphia: Oliver Ditson Company, 1937.

BROOKS, Marian B., and BROWN, Harry A., *Music Education in the Elementary School*. New York: American Book Company, 1946.

BYER, Maude G., *Music Education in Elementary Schools*. San Francisco: Fearon Publishers, 1957.

CARABO-CONE, Madeleine, *The Playground as Music Teacher.* New York: Harper & Brothers, Publishers, 1959.

CARABO-CONE, Madeleine and ROYT, Beatrice. *How To Help Children Learn Music.* New York: Harper & Brothers, Publishers, 1953.

COLEMAN, Jack L., *et al., Music for Exceptional Children.* Evanston, Ill.: Summy-Birchard Company, 1964.

DYKEMA, Peter W., and CUNDIFF, Hannah M. *School Music Handbook.* Boston: C. C. Birchard & Co., 1955.

ELLIOTT, Raymond, *Teaching Music: Methods and Materials for the Elementary Schools.* Columbus, Ohio: Charles E. Merrill Books, Inc., 1960.

ELLISON, Alfred, *Music with Children.* New York: McGraw-Hill Book Company, 1959.

FOX, Lillian M., and HOPKINS, L. Thomas. *Creative School Music.* New York: Silver Burdett Company, 1936.

GINGLEND, David R., and STILES, Winifred E. *Music Activities for Retarded Children.* New York: Abingdon Press, 1965.

GRANT, Parks, *Music for Elementary Teachers.* Second Edition. New York: Appleton-Century-Crofts, Inc., 1960.

HARTSELL, O. M., *Teaching Music in the Elementary School.* Washington, D. C.: Music Educators National Conference, 1963.

HERMANN, Edward J., *Supervising Music in the Elementary School.* Englewood Cliffs, N. J.: Prentice-Hall, Inc., 1965.

HOOD, Marguerite V., and SCHULTZ, E. J. *Learning Music Through Rhythm.* Boston: Ginn and Company, 1949.

HUGHES, Dorothy T., *Rhythmic Games and Dances.* New York: American Book Company, 1942.

HUMPHREYS, Louise, and ROSS, Jerrold. *Interpreting Music Through Movement.* Englewood Cliffs, N. J.: Prentice-Hall, Inc., 1964.

INGRAM, Madeleine D., *Organizing and Directing Children's Choirs.* New York: Abingdon Press, 1959.

JONES, Archie (editor), *Music Education in Action: Basic Principles and Practical Methods.* Boston: Allyn and Bacon, Inc., 1960.

KRONE, Beatrice Perham, and MILLER, Kurt R. *Help Yourselves to Music.* San Francisco: Chandler Publishing Company, 1959.

LANDECK, Beatrice, *Children and Music.* New York: William Sloane Associates, Inc., 1952.

LAWRENCE, Sidney J., *Everyone's Musical.* Evanston, Ill.: Summy-Birchard Company, 1946.

LEONHARD, Charles, *Recreation Through Music.* New York: The Ronald Press Company, 1952.

LEONHARD, Charles, and HOUSE, Robert W. *Foundations and Principles of Music Education.* New York: McGraw-Hill Book Company, 1959.

MADISON, Thurber H. (Chairman), *et al., Basic Concepts in Music Education.* The Fifty-Seventh Yearbook of the National Society of the Study of Education. Chicago: University of Chicago Press, 1958.

MATHEWS, Paul W., *You Can Teach Music.* New York: E. P. Dutton & Co., Inc., 1953.

MARVEL, Lorene, *The Music Consultant at Work.* New York: Bureau of Publications, Teachers College, Columbia University, 1960.

McMILLAN, L. Eileen, *Guiding Children's Growth Through Music.* Boston: Ginn and Company, 1959.

MILLER, Paul Jerome, *Youth Choirs.* New York: Harold Flammer, Inc., 1953.

MORGAN, Hazel N., *Music in American Education.* Washington, D. C.: Music Educators National Conference, 1955.

MUSIC EDUCATORS NATIONAL CONFERENCE, *Music Education for Elementary School Children.* Washington, D. C.: M. E. N. C., 1960.

MURSELL, James L., *Education for Musical Growth.* Boston: Ginn and Company, 1948.

MURSELL, James L., *Music and the Classroom Teacher.* Morristown, N. J.: Silver Burdett Company, 1953.

MURSELL, James L., *Music Education: Principles and Programs.* Morristown, N. J.: Silver-Burdett Company, 1956.

MYERS, Louise K., *Teaching Children Music in the Elementary School.* Third Edition. Englewood Cliffs, N. J.: Prentice-Hall, Inc., 1961.

NATIONAL EDUCATION ASSOCIATION, *Music and Art in the Public*

Schools. Washington, D. C.: National Education Association of the United States, 1963.

NYE, Robert E., and NYE, Vernice T. *Music in the Elementary School.* Second Edition. Englewood Cliffs, N. J.: Prentice-Hall, Inc., 1964.

PIERCE, Anne E., *Teaching Music in the Elementary School.* New York: Holt, Rinehart and Winston, Inc., 1959.

RAEBECK, Lois, and WHEELER, Lawrence. *New Approaches to Music in the Elementary School.* Dubuque, Iowa: Wm. C. Brown Company Publishers, 1964.

RUNKLE, Aleta, and ERIKSEN, Mary LeBow, *Music for Today's Boys and Girls.* Boston: Allyn and Bacon, Inc., 1966.

SAFFRAN, Rosanna B., *First Book of Creative Rhythms.* New York: Holt, Rinehart and Winston, Inc., 1963.

SCHUBERT, Inez, and WOOD, Lucille. *The Craft of Music Teaching.* Morristown, N. J.: Silver Burdett Company, 1964.

SHAFER, Mary S., *Rhythms for Children.* New York: A. S. Barnes, 1938.

SHEEHY, Emma D., *Children Discover Music and Dance.* New York: Holt, Rinehart and Winston, Inc., 1959.

SHEEHY, Emma D., *There's Music in Children.* New York: Holt & Company, 1946.

SLIND, Lloyd H., and DAVIS, D. Evan. *Bringing Music to Children.* New York: Harper & Row, Publishers, 1964.

SNYDER, Alice M., *Creating Music With Children.* New York: Mills Music, Inc., 1957.

SQUIRE, Russel Nelson, *Introduction to Music Education.* New York: Ronald Press Company, 1952.

SWANSON, Bessie, *Music in the Education of Children.* Second Edition. Belmont, Calif.: Wadsworth Publishing Company, Inc., 1964.

SWANSON, Bessie, *Planning Music in the Education of Children.* Belmont, Calif.: Wadsworth Publishing Company, Inc., 1965.

TAUBMAN, Howard, *How to Bring Up Your Child to Enjoy Music.* Garden City, N. Y.: Hanover House, 1958.

THOMPSON, Carl O., and NORDHOLM, Harriet. *Keys to Teaching Elementary School Music.* Minneapolis: Paul A. Schmitt Co., 1949.

Timmerman, Maurine, *Let's Teach Music in the Elementary School*. Evanston, Ill.: Summy-Birchard Company, 1960.

Tooze, Ruth, and Krone, Beatrice. *Literature and Music as Resources for Social Studies*. Englewood Cliffs, N. J.: Prentice-Hall, Inc., 1955.

General education: curriculum, principles and methods

Beaucamp, George A., *Planning the Elementary School Curriculum*. Boston: Allyn and Bacon, Inc., 1956.

Beck, Robert, Cook, Walter and Kearney, Nolan. *Curriculum in the Modern Elementary School*. Second Edition. Englewood Cliffs, N. J.: Prentice-Hall, Inc., 1960.

Burrows, Alvina Treut, *Teaching Children in the Middle Grades*. Boston: D. C. Heath and Company, 1952.

Chasnoff, Robert E. (editor). *Elementary Curriculum*. New York: Pittman Publishing Corporation, 1964.

Crow, Lester D., Crow, Alice, and Murray, Walter (editors), *Teaching in the Elementary School*. New York: Longmans, Green and Co., 1961.

Cunningham, Ruth, *Understanding Group Behavior of Boys and Girls*. New York: Bureau of Publications, Teachers College, Columbia University, 1951.

Fleming, Robert S. (editor), *Curriculum for Today's Boys and Girls*. Columbus, Ohio: Charles E. Merrill Books, Inc., 1963.

Harrison, Raymond H., and Gowin, Lawrence E. *The Elementary Teacher in Action*. San Francisco: Wadsworth Publishing Company, Inc., 1958.

Hurley, Beatrice Davis, *Curriculum for Elementary School Children*. New York: The Ronald Press, 1957.

Jameson, Marshall C., and Hicks, William Vernon. *Elementary School Curriculum*. New York: American Book Company, 1960.

Kelner, Bernard G., *How to Teach in the Elementary School*. New York: McGraw-Hill Book Company, 1958.

Klausmeier, Herbert J., and Dresden, Katharine. *Teaching in* the *Elementary School*. Second Edition. New York: Harper & Brothers, 1962.

LANGDON, Grace, and STOUT, Irving W. *Teaching in the Primary Grades*. New York: The Macmillan Company, 1964.

LEE, J. Murray, and LEE, Doris May. *The Child and His Curriculum*. New York: Appleton-Century-Crofts, Inc., 1958.

MCKIM, Margaret, HANSEN, Carl W., and CARTER, William L. *Learning to Teach in the Elementary School*. New York: The Macmillan Company, 1959.

OHLSEN, Merle M. (editor), *Modern Methods in Elementary Education*. New York: Henry Holt and Company, Inc., 1959.

PETERSON, Dorothy, and HAYDEN, Velma, *Teaching & Learning in the Elementary School*. New York: Appleton-Century-Crofts, Inc., 1961.

POUNDS, Ralph L., and GARRETSON, Robert L. *Principles of Modern Education*. New York: The Macmillan Company, 1962.

RAGAN, William B., *Modern Elementary Curriculum*. Revised Edition. New York: Henry Holt and Company, Inc., 1960.

RAGAN, William B., *Teaching America's Children*. New York: Holt, Rinehart, and Winston, Inc., 1961.

RUCKER, W. Ray, *Curriculum Development in the Elementary School*. New York: Harper & Brothers, Publishers, 1960.

STENDLER, Celia B., *Teaching in the Elementary School*. New York: Harcourt, Brace, 1958.

WARREN, Ruby H., *The Child and His Elementary School World*, Englewood Cliffs, N. J.: Prentice-Hall, Inc., 1957.

Basic music textbooks

Birchard Music Series by Karl Ernst *et al.*
Summy-Birchard Company, Evanston, Ill., 1962.
Books for Kindergarten through eighth grade (Teacher's books for Kindergarten and first grade. Pupil's and teacher's books for grades two to eight).
Recordings available for all books.

Growing With Music by Harry R. Wilson *et al.*
>Prentice-Hall, Inc., Englewood Cliffs, N. J., 1963.
>>Books for grades one through six.
>>Teacher's edition is available for each grade level.
>>Recordings are available for all songs.

Magic of Music, The, by Lorrain E. Watters *et al.*
>Ginn and Company, Boston, 1965.
>>Books for Kindergarten through sixth grade (teacher's books for Kindergarten and first grade. Pupils and teacher's books for grades two to six).
>>Recordings are available for songs in each book.

Making Music Your Own by Beatrice Landeck *et al.*
>Silver Burdett Company, Morristown, N. J., 1965.
>>Books for first through sixth grade.
>>Teacher's edition is available for each grade level.
>>Recordings available for songs in each book.

Music for Living by James L. Mursell *et al.*
>Silver Burdett Company, Morristown, N. J., 1956.
>>I Like the City (1, primer)
>>I Like the Country (1, primer)
>>Music through the Day (T-1)
>>Music in Our Town (2)
>>Music Now and Long Ago (3)
>>Music Near and Far (4)
>>Music in our Country (5)
>>Music Around the World (6)
>>Teacher's edition is available for each grade level.
>>Recordings are available for songs in each book.

Music for Young Americans by Richard C. Berg *et al.*
>American Book Company, New York, 1961.
>>Books for Kindergarten through eighth grade (teacher's books for Kindergarten and first grade. Pupils and teacher's books for grades two to eight).
>>Guide and accompaniments for books two to eight.
>>Recordings are available for songs in each book.

Our Singing World (Enlarged Edition) by Lilla Belle Pitts *et al.*

Ginn and Company, Boston, 1959.

Singing as We Play (Primer I)
Singing All the Day (Primer II)
The Kindergarten Book (T)
The First Grade Book (T)
Singing On Our Way (2)
Singing and Rhyming (3)
Singing Every Day (4)
Singing Together (5)
Singing in Harmony (6)
Singing Juniors (7)
Singing Teen-Agers (8)
Recordings are available for songs in each book.
Teacher's books for Kindergarten and first grade.
Pupils and teacher's books for grades two to six.
Piano accompaniments for books two to six.
Guide and teaching suggestions for Kindergarten-Primary grades.
Guide and teaching suggestions for intermediate grades.

This is Music by William Sur *et al.*

Allyn and Bacon, Inc., Boston, 1961.

Books for Kindergarten through sixth grade.
Teachers editions for each grade level.
Recordings are available for songs in each book.

Together We Sing by Max Krone *et al.*

Follett Publishing Company, Chicago, 1959.

Music Round the Clock (K, 1, 2)
Music Round the Town (K, 1, 2)
Music Through the Year (3, 4)
Music Across the Country (3, 4)
Voices of America (5, 6)
Voices of the World (5, 6)
Music Sounds Afar (7, 8)
Proudly We Sing (7, 8)
Teacher's editions for each book.
Recordings are available for songs in each book.

Addresses of music textbook publishers

ALLYN AND BACON, INC., 150 Tremont Street, Boston, Massachusetts 02111

AMERICAN BOOK COMPANY, 300 Pike Street, Cincinnati, Ohio 45202

FOLLETT PUBLISHING COMPANY, 1010 West Washington Blvd., Chicago, Illinois 60607

GINN AND COMPANY, Statler Building, Boston, Massachusetts 02117

PRENTICE-HALL, INC., Englewood Cliffs, New Jersey 07632

SILVER BURDETT COMPANY, Park Avenue and Columbia Road, Morristown, N. J.

SUMMY-BIRCHARD PUBLISHING COMPANY, 1834 Ridge Avenue, Evanston, Illinois

Basic record series

Adventures in Music (A New Record Library for Elementary Schools). RCA Victor.

> Complete Series, ten volumes—one volume each for grades 1 and 2, two volumes for grades 3-6.
>
> Available in 33⅓ r.p.m., stereo, and 45 r.p.m
>
> A Teacher's Guide, prepared by Gladys Tipton and Eleanor Tipton, is included with each album. Order from the nearest Ginn and Company Sales Office.

Bowmar Orchestral Library, Bowmar Educational Records. 18 albums, each of which includes suggestions to the teacher and wall charts of musical themes.

> Series 1: Bol #51 Animals and Circus, Bol #52 Nature and Make-Believe, Bol # 53 Pictures and Patterns,

Bol #54 Marches, Bol #55 Dances, Part I Bol #56
Dances, Part II, Bol #57 Fairy Tales in Music,
Bol #58 Stories in Ballet and Opera, Bol #59
Legends in Music, Bol #60 Under Many Flags,
Bol #61 American Scenes.

Series 2: Bol #62 Masters in Music, Bol #63 Concert
Matinee, Bol #64 Miniatures in Music, Bol #65
Music, USA, Bol #66 Oriental Scenes, Bol #67
Fantasy in Music, Bol #68 Classroom Concert.

Musical Sound Books by the Sound Book Press Society, Inc.
Selected and annotated by Lillian Baldwin.

Tiny Masterpieces for Very Young Listeners, 114 selec-
tions on twenty 78 r.p.m., 10 inch discs. Records
MSB78301 to MSB78320. For nursery school,
Kindergarten and primary grades.

For Young Listeners, Fifty 78 r.p.m., 10 inch discs.
Records MSB78001 to MSB78051. For intermediate
grades.

Listeners' Library. Three LP records, 33⅓ r.p.m.
Nos. 33100, 33101, and 33102.

Young Listeners' Library. Three LP records, 33⅓
r.p.m., Nos. 33103, 33104 and 33105.

RCA Victor Library for Elementary Schools

Complete series—21 albums (the Rhythm Program—
6 albums; the Listening Program—6 albums; the
Singing Program, 4 albums; Other Albums: Singing
Games, Music at Christmastime, Music of American
Indians, Music for Rhythm Bands, and Patriotic
Songs). Available in 78 r.p.m., 45 r.p.m. "Notes for
Teachers," prepared by Lilla Belle Pitts and Gladys
Tipton is included in the front of each album.
Order from the nearest Ginn and Company sales
office.

Sources of catalogs of educational recordings

BOWMAR EDUCATIONAL RECORDS, INC., 10515 Burbank Blvd., North Hollywood, California

CAPITOL RECORDS DISTRIBUTING CORPORATION (Capitol and Angel Records), Educational Department, 1750 North Vine Street, Hollywood, Calif. 90028

CHILDREN'S MUSIC CENTER, 5373 West Pico Blvd., Los Angeles, Calif. 90019

COLUMBIA RECORDS, INC., Educational Dept., 799 Seventh Ave., New York, New York 10019

DECCA RECORDS, 50 West 57th Street, New York, New York 10019

RUTH EVANS, Childhood Rhythm Records, P. O. Box 132, Forest Park Branch, Springfield, Mass.

EDUCATIONAL RECORD SALES, 157 Chambers Street, New York, N. Y. 10007. Branches Offices: 500 South Douglas St., El Segundo, Calif. and 3300 North Harlem Ave., Chicago, Illinois

FOLKWAYS RECORDS, 163 West 46th Street, New York, New York 10036

GREYSTONE CORPORATION, Educational Activities Division, 100 Sixth Ave., New York, N. Y. 10013 (Children's Record Guild and Young People's Records)

JOHN W. GUNTER, INC., Curriculum Materials, P. O. Box G, San Mateo, Calif.

KEYBOARD JR. PUBLICATIONS, INC., 1346 Chapel St., New Haven, Conn. 06511

MERCURY RECORD CORP., 35 East Wacker Dr., Chicago, Ill. 60601

PHOEBE JAMES RECORDS, Box 286, Verdugo City, California

RADIO CORPORATION OF AMERICA, RCA Victor Record Division, 155 East 24th Street, New York, New York 10010

RHYTHM-TIME RECORDS, P. O. Box 1106, Santa Barbara, California

RHYTHMS PRODUCTIONS, The Cheviot Corporation, 13152 Grant Avenue, Downey, California

SOUND BOOK PRESS SOCIETY, INC., 36 Garth Road, Scarsdale, N. Y., 10583

VOX PRODUCTIONS, INC., 211 East 43rd Street, New York, New York 10017

Sources of classroom instruments and equipment

CHILDREN'S MUSIC CENTER, 5373 West Pico Blvd., Los Angeles, Calif. 90019

> Rhythm instruments, Resonator Bells, Song Bells, Autoharp, Latin-American instruments, Flutophones, Tonettes, Song Flutes, Recorders, Carl Orff instruments.

CONN CORPORATION, 1101 East Beardsley St., Elkhart, Indiana

> Song Flutes, Rhythm instruments.

EDUCATIONAL MUSIC BUREAU, 434 South Wabash, Chicago, Illinois 60605

> Rhythm Band Instruments, Latin-American Instruments, Melody Bells, Resonator Bells, Carl Orff Instruments, Autoharps, Recorders, Flutophones, Tonettes, Song Flutes, Visual Teaching Aids.

GAMBLE HINGED MUSIC Co., 312 South Wabash Ave., Chicago, Illinois 60604

> Rhythm Band Instruments, Tonettes, Song Flutes, Flutophones, Recorders, Tone Bells, Song Bells, Autoharps, Pitchpipes.

FRED GRETSCH MANUFACTURING Co., 218 South Wabash Ave., Chicago, Ill. 60604

> Latin-American instruments.

JOHN W. GUNTER, INC., Curriculum Materials, P. O. Box G, San Mateo, Calif.

> Rhythm Band Instruments, Latin-American Instruments, Autoharps, Resonator Bells.

HARGAIL MUSIC PRESS, 157 West 57th Street, New York, New York 10019
   Imported Recorders and Recorder music.
HARMOLIN, INC., P. O. Box 244, La Jolla, California
   Harmolin, Resonator Bells, Psalteries.
M. HOHNER, INC., Andrews Rd., Hicksville, Long Island, New York 11802
   Resonator Bells, Glockenspiels, Xylophones, Metallophones, Rhythm Band Instruments, Latin-American Instruments, Melodicas, Harmonicas, Recorders.
G. C. JENKINS COMPANY, P. O. Box 149, Decatur, Illinois
   Orchestra Bells.
GEORGE KELISCHEK, 2725 Knox Street, N. E., Atlanta 17, Georgia
   Recorders, Carl Orff Instruments, Instructional materials.
G. F. KITCHING AND COMPANY, INC., 8947 Fairview Ave., Brookfield, Ill. 60513
   Melody Bells, Orchestra Bells, Resonator Bells, Rhythm Instruments, Tuning forks, Tuning bars.
WM. KRATT CO., 988 Johnson Place, Union, New Jersey 07083
   Harmonicas and Pitchpipes.
LYONS BAND INSTRUMENT COMPANY, 223 West Lake St., Chicago, Ill. 60606
   Tonettes, Flutophones, Autoharps, Ukelele, Resonator Bells, Song Bells, Chord Lyre (bells), Orchestra Bells, Latin-American Instruments.
MELODY FLUTE COMPANY, Laurel, Maryland 20810
   Melody Flutes and Recorders.
NATIONAL AUTOHARP SALES COMPANY, P. O. Box 1120, University Station, Des Moines, Iowa 50311
   Autoharps and instructional materials.
OHIO FLOCK-COTE CO., 5713 Euclid Ave., Cleveland, Ohio 44103
   Music-graph flannel boards.
OSCAR SCHMIDT-INTERNATIONAL, INC., 87-101 Ferry Street, Jersey City, New Jersey 07307
   Autoharps and Guitaros.
PERIPOLE PRODUCTS, INC., 51-17 Rockaway Beach Blvd., Far Rockway, Long Island, New York 11691
   Rhythm Band Instruments, Latin-American Instruments,

Song Bells, Resonator Bells, Autoharps, Flutophones, Song Flutes, Tonettes, Recorders, music for all classroom instruments.

RHYTHM BAND, INC., 407-409 Throckmorton St., Fort Worth, Texas 76101

Rhythm Band Instruments, Latin-American Instruments, Autoharps, Flutophones, Tonettes, Song Flutes, Melody Bells, Resonator Bells, Recorders, Fifes, Harmonicas, Ukeleles.

TROPHY PRODUCTS COMPANY, 1278 West 9th Street, Cleveland, Ohio 44113

Flutophones.

VIKING COMPANY, 113 South Edgemont St., Los Angeles, Calif. 90004

Resonator Bells, Music charts.

WALBERG AND AUGE, 31 Mercantile Street, Worcester, Massachusetts 01608

Song Bells, Marimba Bells, Resonator Bells, Autoharps, Rhythm Instruments, Latin-American Instruments, Song Flutes, Tonettes, Flutophones, Recorders.

WILLIS MUSIC COMPANY, 440 Main Street, Cincinnati, Ohio 45202

Rhythm Band Instruments, Melody Bells, Resonator Bells, Flutophones, Song Flutes, Tonettes, Recorders, Autoharps, Pitchpipes, Staff liners.

ZIM-GAR MUSICAL INSTRUMENT CORP., 762 Park Place, Brooklyn, N.Y., 11216

Rhythm Band Instruments, Latin-American Instruments, Autoharps, Zithers, Psalteries, Flutophones, Tonettes, Song Flutes, Resonator Bells, Melody Bells, Orchestra Bells, Xylophones, Stepbells, Recorders, Pitchpipes.

Index

270   **Index**